THE FIFTH MONARCHY MEN

THOMAS VENNER,
ORATOR CONVENTICULORUM REGNI
MILLENARII ET LIBERTINORUM, SEDUCTOR
et CAPITANEUS SEDITIOSOR. ANABAPTISTARUM
ET QVACKERORUM IN CIVITAT. LONDINENS.
Decollatæ in quatuor partes dissectus D. 19. Jan. Anno 1661.

THE
FIFTH
MONARCHY
MEN

P. G. ROGERS

LONDON
Oxford University Press
NEW YORK   TORONTO
1966

Oxford University Press, Ely House, London W. 1

GLASGOW NEW YORK TORONTO MELBOURNE WELLINGTON
CAPE TOWN SALISBURY IBADAN NAIROBI LUSAKA ADDIS ABABA
BOMBAY CALCUTTA MADRAS KARACHI LAHORE DACCA
KUALA LUMPUR HONG KONG

*Printed in Great Britain by
Western Printing Services Ltd, Bristol*

CONTENTS

Illustrations

PREFACE

Thirty-five years ago, when I was a student at the London School of Economics, it was my good fortune to attend a series of lectures given by Professor Harold Laski on the History of Political Ideas. Laski was a very good lecturer, and always worth listening to; but he was perhaps at his best when he was expounding English political thought in the seventeenth century —a period which particularly interested him.

I remember to this day the lecture he gave on the Fifth Monarchy Men. He approached the subject with a delicious blend of academic gravity and flippancy; and it was wholly delightful to hear him discourse profoundly, but also with an amused cynicism, on such favourite topics of the Fifth Monarchy Men as the Little Horn and the Whore of Babylon.

Laski's introduction to the subject was so absorbing that I would dearly have liked to pursue it further; but the harsh exigencies of a degree course forbade any protracted wanderings down sidepaths of History, however delectable the prospect seemed to be.

For many years, therefore, the Fifth Monarchy Men and their aspirations and activities remained to me no more than a blurred memory of a fanatical and fantastic Puritan sect. Then, recently, during researches into English millenarianism in the nineteenth century,[1] I was drawn, ineluctably, back to the seventeenth century and the Fifth Monarchy Men. My old enthusiasm and curiosity were re-awakened, and led me to write the present book. I felt, moreover, that there was some justification for it, since only one book[2] has previously been published on the activities of the sect in general; and that book does not deal with events after 1660.

---

[1] *Battle in Bossenden Wood* (O.U.P. 1961); *The Sixth Trumpeter* (O.U.P. 1963).

[2] L. F. Brown, *The Political Activities of the Baptists and Fifth Monarchy Men in England during the Interregnum* (O.U.P. 1912. Reissued by Burt Franklin, New York 1965).

The illustrations in the present book are reproduced by permission of the Trustees of the British Museum. The portraits of Thomas Venner, John Rogers, and Major-General Harrison are from prints in the Print Room of the British Museum; the title pages of the Fifth Monarchy publications are reproduced from the originals in the Thomason collection in the British Museum Library.

18 March 1965   PHILIP ROGERS

1

THE CULT OF THE MILLENNIUM

To be or not to be: that is the question.
Whether 'tis nobler in the mind to suffer
The slings and arrows of outrageous fortune,
Or to take arms against a sea of troubles,
And by opposing end them? ...

HAMLET'S soliloquy poses a perennial problem that has been answered down the centuries by different individuals and nations according to temperament and circumstance. Nations no less than individuals may tend, at certain periods in their development, through sheer exhaustion or some other cause, passively to 'suffer the slings and arrows of outrageous fortune' rather than actively to confront the ills which assail them. Then, for solace in present misery, the tendency is to look ahead to some future bliss, when by divine intervention the righteous shall come into their own and the oppressors shall be cast down.

It is not surprising, in view of the persecution and vicissitudes which the Jews suffered after the break-up of the ancient kingdom of Solomon, that this tendency is clearly defined at different periods of their history. In 168 B.C. the fortunes of the oppressed people seemed at their lowest ebb. Antiochus IV Epiphanes, the ruler of Syria, persecuted them fanatically and desecrated the temple in Jerusalem. It was at this time of trouble that the prophet Daniel tried to bring consolation to his suffering people. In Chapter VII of the book in the Bible which bears his name is recounted what the prophet saw in a dream:

1. In the first year of Belshazzar king of Babylon Daniel had a dream and visions of his head upon his bed: then he wrote the dream, and told the sum of the matters.

2. Daniel spake and said, I saw in my vision by night, and, behold, the four winds of the heaven strove upon the great sea.

3. And four great beasts came up from the sea, diverse one from another.

4. The first was like a lion, and had eagle's wings: I beheld till the wings thereof were plucked, and it was lifted up from the earth, and made stand upon the feet as a man, and a man's heart was given to it.

5. And behold another beast, a second, like to a bear, and it raised up itself on one side, and it had three ribs in the mouth of it between the teeth of it: and they said thus unto it, Arise, devour much flesh.

6. After this I beheld, and lo another, like a leopard, which had upon the back of it four wings of a fowl; the beast had also four heads; and dominion was given to it.

7. After this I saw in the night visions, and behold a fourth beast, dreadful and terrible, and strong exceedingly; and it had great iron teeth: it devoured and brake in pieces, and stamped the residue with the feet of it: and it was diverse from all the beasts that were before it; and it had ten horns.

8. I considered the horns, and, behold, there came up among them another little horn, before whom there were three of the first horns plucked up by the roots: and, behold, in this horn were eyes like the eyes of man, and a mouth speaking great things.

9. I beheld till the thrones were cast down, and the Ancient of days did sit, whose garment was white as snow, and the hair of his head like the pure wool: his throne was like the fiery flame, and his wheels as burning fire.

10. A fiery stream issued and came forth from before him: thousand thousands ministered unto him, and ten thousand times ten thousand stood before him: the judgment was set, and the books were opened.

11. I beheld then because of the voice of the great words which the horn spake: I beheld even till the beast was slain, and his body destroyed, and given to the burning flame.

12. As concerning the rest of the beasts, they had their dominion taken away: yet their lives were prolonged for a season and time.

13. I saw in the night visions, and, behold, one like the Son of man came with the clouds of heaven, and came to the Ancient of days, and they brought him near before him.

14. And there was given him dominion, and glory, and a kingdom, that all people, nations, and languages, should serve him: his dominion is an everlasting dominion, which shall not pass away, and his kingdom that which shall not be destroyed.

15. I Daniel was grieved in my spirit in the midst of my body, and the visions of my head troubled me.

16. I came near unto one of them that stood by, and asked him the truth of all this. So he told me, and made me know the interpretation of the things.

17. These great beasts, which are four, are four kings, which shall arise out of the earth.

18. But the saints of the most High shall take the kingdom, and possess the kingdom for ever, even for ever and ever.

19. Then I would know the truth of the fourth beast, which was diverse from all the others, exceeding dreadful, whose teeth were of iron, and his nails of brass; which devoured, brake in pieces, and stamped the residue with his feet;

20. And of the ten horns that were in his head, and of the other which came up, and before whom three fell; even of that horn that had eyes, and a mouth that spake very great things, whose look was more stout than his fellows.

21. I beheld, and the same horn made war with the saints, and prevailed against them;

22. Until the Ancient of days came, and judgment was given to the saints of the most High; and the time came that the saints possessed the kingdom.

23. Thus he said, The fourth beast shall be the fourth kingdom upon earth, which shall be diverse from all kingdoms, and shall devour the whole earth, and shall tread it down, and break it in pieces.

24. And the ten horns out of this kingdom are ten kings that shall arise; and another shall rise after them; and he shall be diverse from the first, and he shall subdue three kings.

25. And he shall speak great words against the most High, and shall wear out the saints of the most High, and think to change times and laws, and they shall be given into his hand until a time and times and the dividing of time.

26. But the judgment shall sit, and they shall take away his dominion, to consume and to destroy it unto the end.

27. And the kingdom and dominion, and the greatness of the kingdom under the whole heaven, shall be given to the people of the saints of the most High, whose kingdom is an everlasting kingdom, and dominions shall serve and obey him.

To Daniel and his contemporaries the fourth beast mentioned in the dream was the Syrian kingdom of Antiochus Epiphanes, which had followed the other beasts—the empires of the Babylonians, the Persians, and the Greeks. This fourth beast would be overthrown in the fullness of time, and then the saints of the most High, the Jews, would take the kingdom and possess it for ever.

This, however, was a prophecy unfulfilled; for though there was a short-lived Jewish revival under Judas Maccabaeus, there came again times of desolation and oppression, when the Jews fell under the domination of Rome. During this renewal of subjection to a foreign power the Jews sought solace in the expectation that a messiah would deliver them, and usher in the promised age. But once again expectations were not fulfilled, and the final crushing of Jewish resistance and the dispersion of the people which took place in A.D. 135 seemed so final that Jewish belief in the ultimate restoration of Israel, though never extinguished, was dimmed for centuries to come.

But the doctrine of the millennium, the time of fulfilment when the just should come into their own, lived on among the early Christians. These suffered intermittent persecution, which sometimes reached savage proportions, until A.D. 311 when the Emperor Constantine issued his edict of toleration. During the three centuries of suffering the early Christians, like the Jews, looked for comfort and strength to an imminent cataclysm, when the evil rulers of the world would be overthrown, and the persecuted would enter into their due and rightful inheritance.

The most remarkable exposition of this belief is to be found in the Book of Revelation, which is generally thought to have been written about A.D. 93 during a wave of persecution instigated by the Emperor Domitian. There are many resemblances between Revelation and the Book of Daniel in the Old Testament, and this is particularly apparent in Revelation, Chapter XIII, where, as in Daniel, the evil kingdoms of the world are symbolized as monstrous beasts with horns, and their destruction ushers in the reign of the just. Chapter XIII of Revelation relates, for example:

1. And I stood upon the sand of the sea, and saw a beast rise up out of the sea, having seven heads and ten horns, and upon his horns ten crowns, and upon his heads the name of blasphemy.
2. And the beast which I saw was like unto a leopard, and his feet were as the feet of a bear, and his mouth as the mouth of a lion: and the dragon gave him his power, and his seat, and great authority.
3. And I saw one of his heads as it were wounded to death; and his

deadly wound was healed: and all the world wondered after the beast.

4. And they worshipped the dragon which gave power unto the beast: and they worshipped the beast, saying, Who is like unto the beast? who is able to make war with him?

5. And there was given unto him a mouth speaking great things and blasphemies; and power was given unto him to continue forty and two months.

6. And he opened his mouth in blasphemy against God, to blaspheme his name, and his tabernacle, and them that dwell in heaven.

7. And it was given unto him to make war with the saints, and to overcome them: and power was given him over all kindreds, and tongues, and nations. . . .

When the persecution of Christianity in the Roman Empire ended, and the Church consolidated itself, its leaders came to disapprove of the literal interpretation of the prophecies in Daniel and Revelation, for these tended to have unsettling effects on the established order, since they induced instability among the more impressionable members of the flock. Thus from the fifth century A.D. onwards official doctrine taught that the apocalyptic visions of Daniel and Revelation were not to be taken literally, but were instead to be interpreted as allegories of a spiritual transformation of men's souls.

Such refined intellectual reasoning could not, however, be expected to appeal to the illiterate emotional masses; and intermittently, during the Middle Ages, especially at times when economic misery and political oppression prevailed in Europe, the old beliefs in a divine upheaval, resulting in the righting of wrongs and the entry of the just into the promised millennium, were fanned into vigorous life again.

As the Middle Ages developed, changes in economic and social conditions took place which, from the eleventh century onwards, encouraged the growth of millenarian ideas in various parts of Europe. As a result of the increase in population in some areas, a class of peasants with no land, or with insufficient land to maintain them, came into being. Moreover, the decay of the manorial system loosened customary bonds between peasant and lord which, even if they had pressed heavily on the unfree peasants, had also constituted some measure of protection against rapacious lords.

The development of commerce and industry encouraged the growth of towns; and to these many of the landless and discontented peasants gravitated, in search of a better life. But in the towns, under the medieval gild system, a society developed in which many found themselves poverty-stricken and underprivileged, in contrast to the master-craftsmen and merchants who formed a rich and powerful minority.

Such rural and urban conditions, of rich and poor, of privileged and underprivileged, were fertile ground for the resurgence of the age-old millenarian doctrine of hope that the day of the poor and oppressed was at hand, and afforded opportunity for agitators and demagogues to set themselves up as the prophets of the coming new order.

In the thirteenth century, for example, it was widely believed that the Holy Roman Emperor, Frederick II, would be the instrument by which the golden age would be ushered in; and even his death in 1250 did not extinguish hopes that he would one day reappear to carry out his great work.

A century and a half later John Hus in Bohemia, in his attacks against the papacy and the clergy, gained many followers called Hussites. Among these a radical movement developed, the members of which were called Taborites, who believed that the millennium was near, when all social and economic inequality would disappear, and private property and all forms of human authority would be abolished. These egalitarian and anarchistic doctrines led to a conflict between the conservatively-minded Hussites and the Taborites; and after defeat in battle in 1434, the Taborites, as an organized movement with revolutionary aims, decayed.

Their millenarian conceptions lingered on, however, and reappeared in Germany in the early sixteenth century when Thomas Muntzer, championing the cause of the rebellious German peasants in Thuringia, proclaimed that the coming of the millennium was near, and must be hastened by force of arms.

Muntzer and his followers were suppressed, and he himself was put to death in 1525; but once again the failure of a millenarian revolt and the death of its prophet did not stop a recurrence of the belief, and the willingness to fight and die for it. It reappeared in the sixteenth century in the form of a militant revolutionary Anabaptism, which led to one of the most bizarre and calamitous episodes in European history. This was the short-lived regime of the Anabaptists in Münster in Westphalia. In 1532 John Mathias, a baker of Haarlem in Holland, declared that he was the high priest of God, and preached that Christ would shortly appear to inaugurate the millennium, when the just would reign supreme with him for one thousand years. Mathias found willing disciples, and one of these, John Buckhold, a butcher of Leyden, he sent to Münster to spread the new gospel there.

Buckhold did his work so well that Mathias later joined him, and by 1534 their followers had become so numerous that they were able to take complete control of the town. At once a new regime was inaugurated, in preparation for Christ's second coming, and credulous peasants from the surrounding neighbourhood flocked into Münster to join the Lord's elect. Meanwhile, however, the Bishop of Münster had been assembling forces to retake the city, to which they now laid siege. In a fanatical foray against the besiegers Mathias was killed, and was succeeded as leader by Buckhold.

Despite, or perhaps because of the severity of the siege, Buckhold now began to indulge in grotesque extravagances. He proclaimed that polygamy was lawful, and promptly took to himself three wives, one of whom was the widow of Mathias. He had himself invested as king, attired himself in silken robes, and wore a crown of gold. He proclaimed himself the 'King of Justice, the King of the New Jerusalem', and assured his now flagging followers that help would come from neighbouring Holland to enable the siege to be raised. After this all wicked and refractory princes would be subdued, and the peaceful reign of justice established on earth.

The help did not come, however, and by February 1535 starvation faced the besieged. Murmurings of revolt began to be heard, and Elizabeth, one of the 'king's' wives, was implicated. Her punishment was swift and terrible. She was brought to the market-place; and in the presence of the other royal wives and the terrified populace the 'king' himself struck off her head. Intimidated by this demonstration of fanatical ruthlessness the starving people were forced further to endure their miseries—but a few weeks later, through an act of treachery, one of the city gates was opened, the besiegers entered, the 'king' and his chief lieutenant were captured, and the regime of the new Jerusalem came to an end.

On 20 January 1536 Buckhold and his chief accomplices were brought back to Münster, after having been paraded through Westphalia; and on 23 January they were put to death. Buckhold was tied to a stake, and according to a seventeenth-century chronicler of the event,[1] for a whole hour his body was pulled and lacerated by two executioners armed with red-hot pincers. At length, to put him out of his misery, he was run through with a sword. His companions were similarly dealt with; and their mutilated corpses were later put into iron baskets which were suspended from a church tower as a grisly warning to any persons who might be contemplating a revival of revolt against the established order.

John Buckhold and his followers were called Anabaptists by their contemporaries because they rejected infant baptism, and therefore required their followers to be re-baptised. It was, however, their other doctrines, bound up with their belief in the imminence of the millennium, which caused the greatest scandal and horror. Indeed, for many years to come the word Anabaptist was to be used loosely to describe religious fanatics and desperadoes of all kinds, and it conjured up in the mind of the law-abiding the most terrible images of excess and disorder.

Despite the opprobrium and severe repression which the Münster episode brought on the head of millenarians, the belief in the second coming of 'King Jesus' and the inauguration of the rule of the elect—the 'saints'—was not extinguished, and prophets of the thousand-year reign continued to appear from time to time. One of these was William Hacket, who was born at Oundle in Northamptonshire in the early part of the reign of Queen Elizabeth.

Though he was born of humble parents and failed in his early manhood to obtain any higher employment than that of servant, he managed to attract a rich widow, married her, and then began a course of riotous living. During this period of profligacy he committed many excesses, and one day, during a drunken quarrel with a schoolmaster in an Oundle inn he bit the unfortunate man's nose right off, and then in his rage ate it. When his drunken

---

[1] A. Ross, *A View of all Religions in the World* (London 1675).

rage had passed, the repentant Hacket was overwhelmed by the enormity of the crime he had committed. He forthwith renounced his evil way of life and then veered to the other extreme, claiming that God's truth had been revealed to him, and that he had been given a divine commission to prepare for Christ's second coming.

Hacket attracted a few disciples locally, and then went with one of them to York to spread his tidings. The city authorities did not react as he had hoped, and instead of being received with joy, he and his follower were whipped out of York and told not to return. Undaunted they went to Leicester, only to experience the same treatment there, and Hacket then decided to try his fortunes in London.

There, using a house near Broken Wharf, off Upper Thames Street, as his headquarters, he sent out two of his supporters, Edward Coppinger and Henry Arthington, who appear to have been of some social standing and were described by contemporaries as gentlemen. They were ordered to proclaim to the City of London that Christ Jesus, who was in Walker's House by Broken Wharf, had come to judge the earth. Both men gladly obeyed, and strode along the streets towards Cheapside announcing their message and crying out aloud, 'Repent, England, Repent!'

Soon a large crowd was following them, and by the time they reached Cheapside they could advance no further because of the press of people. By the cross in Cheapside, however, stood a cart, and so they clambered into this, and once again began repeating their exhortations to the crowd. The message was ill-received, and the two messengers deemed it wise to escape. They managed to climb down from the cart and slip into a nearby tavern, and leaving this by the back door they returned through the back streets to Broken Wharf. 'This strange accident,' John Stow wrote in his Chronicle, 'beeing quickly blowne through the City, all was in a buzze, and a kind of astonishment'—and the result was that in the afternoon Hacket and his two heralds were brought before members of the Privy Council for questioning. It was decided that Hacket should be put on trial, and on 21 July 1590 he was found guilty of having spoken 'divers most false and traiterous words' against Queen Elizabeth, and to have defaced a painting of her by thrusting an iron bar through that part of the painting which did represent the brest and heart of the Queenes Majesty'.

Condemned to death on 28 July, Hacket was brought from Newgate to the place of execution in Cheapside, by the cross where his disciples had addressed the crowd. Completely obsessed to the last by his millenarian ideas, he cried out insistently as he was dragged on a hurdle through the streets: 'Jehovah! Messiah! Jehovah! Messiah!' and 'Look! Look! How the heavens open wide and the Son of God cometh down to deliver me!'

Before he was hanged he was exhorted to pray for God's and the Queen's forgiveness; but instead, as Stow recounts, he 'fell to rayling and cursing of Her Majestie most villainously, and then began a most blasphemous and execrable prayer against the divine majesty of God. They had much adoe to get him up the ladder, where he was hanged, and after bowelled and quartered.'[2]

Not all the millenarians were as wild as Hacket and his followers. In an age when biblical exegesis attracted magnetically the most brilliant minds, sober and learned examination of the prophecies relating to Christ's second coming were not lacking. One of the earliest of such attempts to resolve the apocalyptic mysteries was made by Joseph Mede. Born in 1586 in Essex, he graduated at Cambridge and became famous for his erudition. He firmly believed that the millennium was near, and that it would be preceded by the resurrection of all the saints and martyrs. Mede was a gentle scholar, and his interpretation of the second coming was entirely pacific, but later visionaries were to quote and use it for their own more militant ends.

I dare boldly say [remarked Fuller in his *Worthies of England* (1662)] that the furious factors for the Fifth Monarchy hath driven that nail which Master Mede did first enter, farther than he ever intended it; and doing it with such violence that they split the truths round about it. Thus, when ignorance begins to build on that foundation which learning hath laid, no wonder if there be no uniformity in such a mongrel fabric. . . .

Robert Maton, born at Tidworth in 1607, was another scholarly divine who elaborated millenary ideas. He did so,

---

[2] E. Howes, *Annales, or a Generall Chronicle of England Begun by John Stow, continued and augmented with Matters Foraigne and Domestique, Ancient and Moderne, unto the end of this present yeere* (1631), pp. 761–2.

however, without giving them publicity, until the advent of the
Civil War made him more adventurous. In 1642 he produced
*Israel's Redemption, or the Propheticall History of Our Saviour's
Kingdom on Earth*; and *Gog and Magog, or the Battle of the
Great Day of God Almightie*. Maton's ardent advocacy of mil-
lenarian ideas provoked controversy, and this was carried further
by the publication, also in 1642, of the clearest, boldest, and most
detailed exposition of the beliefs so far. The author, Henry Archer,
formerly a preacher at the church of All Hallows in Lombard
Street, produced it under the following title:

The Personall
Reign of
Christ
Upon Earth

In a Treatise wherin is fully and largely
laid open and proved, That *Jesus Christ* together
with the Saints, shall visibly possesse a
Monarchical State and Kingdom in
this World.
Which sheweth,

1. That there shall be such a Kingdome.
2. The Manner of it.
3. The Duration of it.
4. The Time when it is to begin.

Quoting freely from the Book of Daniel, Archer declared
that four monarchies had existed—the Babylonian/Assyrian,
the Mede/Persian, the Greek, and the Roman. After the downfall of the fourth, the Roman monarchy, a fifth would arise, that
of Christ. The Saviour would come visibly from heaven to set
this up, but after he had 'put his kingdome into forme' he would
withdraw to heaven again and leave its government to the saints,
until his third coming after a thousand years, when the Day of
Judgement would begin, and all the wicked would be destroyed.

Archer was naturally concerned to determine the precise date
of Christ's second coming, when the thousand-year reign would
be inaugurated. He considered that this would happen when
the fourth monarchy had finally expired; and so he turned to
Daniel, Chapter VII, for he concluded that the answer to the
question lay in the interpretation of the prophet's dream.

The fourth beast which Daniel had seen, Archer said, had ten horns. Moreover, 'there came up among them another little horn, before whom there were three of the first horns plucked up by the roots' (verse 8). The ten horns, Archer declared, were the kingdoms which had arisen out of the western part of the Roman monarchy, or empire. The 'fearefull little Horne', however, which came up among them was the Papacy, 'because of its base works'—since it made war with the saints, and prevailed against them. (Daniel vii. 21.)

The 'Little Horn' was, nevertheless, to be doomed after 'a time, times, and an half' (Daniel xii. 7); and from Revelation (x. 2) Archer deduced that by this cryptic phrase a period of forty-two months was meant.[3] Further, from Revelation (xii. 6) he fancied that he had corroboration that this period was equivalent to 1260 days.[4] The biblical day, however, signified a year; so that if the 'Little Horn' or Papacy was to prevail over the saints from the beginning of the ten kingdoms in Western Europe for 1260 years, when that period ended the fifth monarchy or reign of the saints would begin.

So, Archer declared, 'the great question is, when the ten kingdoms and Papacy began in Europe?' He conceded that historians differed somewhat in their calculations, by four or five years, but he asserted that in the general opinion it was about A.D. 400–6 that the Bishop of Rome began to assume 'usurped powers', and about this time too that some of the ten kingdoms in Europe began to arise. 'Let us', said Archer, 'reckon it 406 when it begun . . . then add to 406 the 1260, and it maketh 1666, which is the time made the number of the Beast (Revelation xiii. 18),[5] that is, the Papacies duration. . . .'

However, there was, Archer went on, an alternative method of reckoning. The conversion of the Jews was to precede the reign

---

[3] 'But the court which is without the temple leave out, and measure it not; for it is given unto the Gentiles: and the holy city shall they tread under foot forty and two months.'

[4] 'And the woman fled into the wilderness, where she hath a place prepared of God, that they should feed her there a thousand two hundred and threescore days.'

[5] 'Here is wisdom. Let him that hath understanding count the number of the beast: for it is the number of a man; and his number is Six hundred threescore and six.'

of the saints, and that, according to Daniel (xii. 11),[6] would be 1290 days after 'the abomination that maketh desolate' was set up. The abomination in question, Archer said, was set up in the reign of the Roman Emperor, Julian the Apostate, 'who reigned in the yeare of our Lord 360 or 366, and set up Heathenisme, that abomination. . . .' If, then, 1290 was added to 360 or 366 the dates 1650 and 1656 resulted, and one or other of these two dates was therefore the time appointed for the conversion of the Jews. From then onwards however, for forty-five years, the twelve tribes were to suffer great troubles (Daniel xii. 12);[7] but then Christ would come to establish his kingdom, which was to last for a thousand years. 'So', Archer confidently concluded, 'it is likely that Christ's comming from Heaven, and raysing the dead, and beginning his kingdome, and the thousand years, will bee about the yeare of our Lord 1700, for it is to be about fortie-five yeares after 1650 or 1656.'

Archer had done his painstaking best to show when the millennium could be expected to begin. That happy consummation was, however, still half a century distant. What was to be done in the meantime, during the period of waiting? Archer was not unmindful that this question might be raised by his readers, and he tried to answer it in the last paragraphs of his treatise. 'What use should we make of all this doctrine about Christ's kingdom?' he asked, and replied that an answer to that problem also could be found in the scriptures. These taught that God's people should look for the kingdom and long for it to come. They could not hasten its coming, yet they themselves might hasten towards it by eschewing all evil and by making themselves ready for it.

This was a tame conclusion to draw from such exciting doctrines; and other, bolder spirits were soon to place their own more violent construction upon them. In doing this they were both stimulated and strengthened by the political convulsions which England was to undergo during the eighteen years which followed the publication of Archer's book.

---

[6] 'And from the time that the daily sacrifice shall be taken away, and the abomination that maketh desolate set up, there shall be a thousand two hundred and ninety days.'

[7] 'Blessed is he that waiteth, and cometh to the thousand three hundred and five and thirty days.'

2

TEETERING AND TUMBLING AFFAIRS

WHEN, in August 1642, King Charles set up his standard at Nottingham and thus made inevitable the outbreak of the Civil War, he enjoyed one special and very considerable advantage over his opponents. That was the divinity which hedged a king, the aura of sanctity which prevented many of his subjects taking arms against him, even if they disapproved of his policies. For this reason again, in 1647, after Charles had been decisively defeated in the fighting, and had been handed over to the Parliamentary leaders by the Scots to whom he had surrendered in May 1646, there was a widespread reluctance to take extreme measures against him.

By his devious manoeuvres and tergiversations, however, the king dissipated what chances were left to him of remaining on the throne. More and more people came to regard him as untrustworthy, and as a hindrance to be removed before the future government of the country could be established on a firm basis. These feelings were reinforced when Charles, in November 1647, escaped from Hampton Court, where he had been kept under close surveillance while the leaders of the army and of Parliament debated what terms should be offered him.

Charles fled from Hampton Court to Carisbrooke Castle in the Isle of Wight, and there he reopened negotiations with the Scots, which led to their invading England in 1648 in his support, and the outbreak of the second Civil War. The Scots were defeated by Cromwell and driven back to their own country; the revolts in England were put down; and now Charles had to face the bitter animosity which his conduct had aroused, particularly in the ranks of the army.

One of his most implacable opponents was Thomas Harrison. Harrison came of a middle-class family in Newcastle-under-

Lyme, Staffordshire, and after his schooling had served as a clerk to a solicitor in Clifford's Inn, London. When the Civil War broke out he joined the bodyguard of the Earl of Essex on the parliamentary side, showed great courage and ability in several major battles, and obtained steady promotion, reaching the rank of colonel in 1645.

Harrison was not only a tough soldier, however. He was also a deeply religious man, and at some time, probably during the Civil War, he became a convert to the doctrines of the English millenarians. These were already beginning to be known as the Fifth Monarchy Men because of their insistence that with Christ's coming to inaugurate the reign of the saints the fourth monarchy would end and the fifth begin. To a man of Harrison's fanatical temperament, now passionately imbued with this belief, the machinations of Charles Stuart were doubly damned —first, because they were evil in themselves; secondly, because they were deferring the rule of Christ and his elect.

Already in 1647 when the Army was encamped near London with its headquarters at Putney, it was evident that Fifth Monarchy doctrines had made a considerable impact on some of the higher-ranking officers. For instance, during a debate on 29 October Lieutenant-General Goffe discoursed on the apocalyptic writings, and asserted that Christ and his saints had to destroy Antichrist or the rule of iniquity, during the last days. Two other officers, Colonel Rainborough and Colonel Nathaniel Rich, also revealed strong Fifth Monarchy leanings in their support of proposals to end the monarchy and inaugurate the rule of the saints.

As for Colonel Harrison, at a meeting of the Council of Officers at Putney on 11 November, he vehemently declared that the king was a 'man of blood', who should be brought to trial. Cromwell, who was also present at the meeting, spoke against such harsh courses, and quoted biblical precedents for the exercise of clemency. Harrison was for the moment overruled; but he maintained his convictions sturdily.

On 15 December 1648, after the second Civil War had ended, the Army leaders decided that Charles, the instigator of the renewed conflict, should be brought to Windsor Castle; and none other than Colonel Harrison was sent to bring him there from Hurst Castle on the Solent, to which place Charles had been

transferred from Carisbrooke. Harrison travelled down to Hurst
Castle to make arrangements for the king's transfer; and his
arrival, late at night, on 17 December, awoke fears among
Charles' attendants that the visitor had come on a mission of
murder, for it had long been rumoured that certain elements in
the Army wished to resolve the problem of the future of the
monarchy by the drastic means of assassination. However, the
fears of Charles and his attendants proved unfounded, for
Harrison, having made his arrangements, departed again without having established any contact with King Charles.

On 20 December Harrison waited near Farnham for the
arrival of the party escorting the king; and what happened
afterwards was recounted by Sir Thomas Herbert, Groom of
the Chamber to King Charles:

From Alesford [Alresford] the King pass'd to Farnham, betwixt
which two towns . . . another troop of horse was in good order
drawn up, by which His Majesty pass'd. It was to bring up the rear.
In the head of it was the captain [Harrison], gallantly mounted and
armed; a velvet monteir [hunter's cap with ear-flaps] was on his
head, a new buff-coat upon his back, and a crimson silk scarf about
his waist richly-fringed; who as the King pass'd by with an easie
pace (as delighted to see men well hors'd and arm'd), the captain
gave the King a bow with his head all a-Soldade [in military
manner], which His Majesty requited. This was the first time the
King saw that captain. . . .

King Charles asked Herbert who the captain was, and being
told,

The King view'd him more narrowly, and fix'd his eyes so steddily
upon him as made the major [sic] abash'd, and fall back to his
troop sooner than probably he intended. The King said he looked
like a soldier; and that his aspect was good, and found him not
such a one as was represented; and that, having some judgement in
faces, if he had observ'd him so well before, he should not have
harbour'd that ill opinion of him. . . .

During the night after this meeting with Harrison the King was
lodged in a private house in Farnham, and just before taking
supper he noticed Harrison at the end of the room, talking to
another officer.

The King [Herbert recounted] beckoned to him with his hand to come nearer him; which he did with due reverence. The King then taking him by his arm, drew him aside towards the window, where for half an hour or more they discoursed together; and amongst other things the King minded him of the information concerning him, which if true, rendered him an enemy in the worst sense to his person; to which the major in his vindications assured His Majesty that what was so reported of him was not true; what he had said he might repeat, that the law was equally obliging to great and small, and that justice had no respect to persons, or words to that purpose; which His Majesty finding affectedly spoken, and to no good end, he left off further communication with him and went to supper.[1]

Charles was right in thinking that Harrison's blunt words were spoken to no good end; for Harrison, who had long demanded that the King be brought to justice, was now supported by Ireton and other influential Army leaders, and these at last carried the day. The result was the trial of King Charles in Westminster Hall by the so-called High Court of Justice, of which Harrison was a member, and the execution of the King on 30 January 1649.

With the man of blood disposed of, Harrison and his fellow Fifth Monarchists fondly supposed that the way now lay clear to prepare for the inauguration of the millennium, the rule of the saints. That this opinion was shared in the provinces was revealed in February 1649 by the presentation of a petition from Norfolk to General Fairfax and the Army leaders. The petition was as follows:

Certain
Quaeres
humbly presented
In way of Petition
By many Christian People, dispersed abroad
throughout the County of Norfolk and City of Norwich,
To the serious and grave Consideration and Debate
of His Excellency
The Lord General,
and
Of the General Council of War.

---

[1] Sir Thomas Herbert, *Memoirs of the Two Last Years of the Reign of King Charles I* (London 1839), pp. 139–42.

The petitioners, referring to the books of Daniel and Revelation, stated that the Fifth Monarchy was due to succeed the fourth, and then the 'people called by Christ' would exercise dominion over the whole world till Christ came in person to rule over the kingdom. The petitioners asked Fairfax and the Council to further this design by setting up a suitable Government of godly men in England to begin with—in so doing they would be 'the Saints nursing fathers'. But otherwise, how could it be lawful to 'patch up the old worldly government'? Moreover, the petitioners concluded, how dangerous it would be to keep Christ from his throne!

It must be said that the train of recent events in England had seemed to the petitioners and to like-minded men, auspicious. In December 1648 Colonel Pride with his soldiers had 'purged' what remained of the Long Parliament. The truncated remnant, the Rump,[2] consisting of members commonly labelled Independents (that is, men who opposed the hierarchical form of church organization favoured by the Anglicans and Presbyterians)[3] had appointed the High Court of Justice; and after the trial and execution of the King it was this small and quite unrepresentative body which abolished the monarchy, proclaimed the Commonwealth, and established a Council of State as the Government.

---

[2] The Rump's nominal roll seems to have been, at its maximum, 209; but attendances fell far short of this, fluctuating in general, except for special occasions, from 30 to 80. (Brunton and Pennington, *Members of the Long Parliament* (London 1954), pp. 41–42).

[3] The word 'Independent' in a political sense came into use during the Civil War to denote the more radical group in Parliament. The researches of J. H. Hexter (*Reappraisals in History*, London 1961), and G. Yule (*The Independents in the English Civil War*, Cambridge 1958), have shown, however, that the term 'Independent' needs to be used with a good deal of caution and qualification. The Independents were not a homogeneous political group, and numbered in their ranks men who were elders of the Presbyterian Church established by Parliament, as well as others who were neither pure Independents nor orientated towards any cause other than their own advancement. Nevertheless, genuine Independents constituted the core of the group; and the concept of the autonomy of each local religious congregation was basic to true Independency.

However, the Rump itself continued to sit as a 'Parliament', and aroused increasing hostility because of its sterile debates and evident determination to cling to power. Harrison, who in 1650 had been advanced to the rank of major-general, and was a member of the Council of State, was disillusioned with the existing system of government because of its failure to measure up to his millenary expectations. He therefore urged Cromwell to inaugurate a new regime in which government would be carried on exclusively by men chosen for their moral and religious qualifications.

Cromwell was not altogether out of sympathy with Harrison's conception of government. He had a genuine liking for 'godly' men, though his common sense made him recoil swiftly from any extravagances of belief. Like the army as a whole, he was tired of the Rump and its posturings; and, in short, he was prepared to try whether government by the saints, as envisaged by Harrison, was practicable.

The breaking-point for Cromwell came on 20 April 1653, when he heard that members of the Rump were preparing to pass a bill which would, in effect, prolong their existence indefinitely. Cromwell, who himself was a member, went down at once to the Parliament House, accompanied by some thirty musketeers. Leaving the soldiers outside, he entered the chamber and sat down. After he had listened for some time to the debate he rose, and according to one eye-witness, Bulstrode Whitelocke, told his fellow members that 'they had sat long enough . . . that some of them were whore-masters . . . that others of them were drunkards, and some corrupt and unjust men and scandalous to the profession of the Gospel, and that it was not fit that they should sit as a Parliament any longer. . . .'[4]

According to another eye-witness, Algernon Sidney, Cromwell remarked: 'Perhaps you think this is not parliamentary language; I confess it is not, neither are you to expect any such from me!'

After putting on his hat he walked up and down the House and continued bitterly to chide the members. Then, beckoning to Harrison, he cried out: 'Call them in!' whereupon Harrison

---

[4] B. Whitelocke, *Memorials of the English Affairs* (London 1732), p. 554.

fetched in the musketeers under Lieutenant-Colonel Worsley.
Cromwell then pointed to the Speaker, and said to Harrison:
'Fetch him down!' Harrison went to the Speaker, and asked
him to leave his seat. The Speaker, however, sat still and did
nothing; and this caused Cromwell to repeat angrily: 'Take him
down!' According to Algernon Sidney, Harrison thereupon 'went
and pulled the Speaker by the gowne, and he came downe'.
Cromwell now walked to the table where the mace lay, and gave
the order: 'Take away these baubles!' The soldiers obediently
removed the mace, and cleared the House; and this having
been done the door was locked and the key and the mace taken
away for safe keeping. The days of the Rump, for the time being,
were ended.[5]

Another contemporary chronicler of the momentous event,
Edmund Ludlow, said that Cromwell, when chiding the members, told them roundly that 'the Lord had done with them, and
had chosen other instruments for the carrying on his work, that
were more worthy'.[6] The Lord might well have chosen the new
instruments; but the great problem was to devise some means by
which they might be singled out and called to begin their great
work. The problem might be difficult, but advice was not wanting; and of all those who offered Cromwell guidance in the
matter, the most eloquent and persistent was John Rogers.

He had been born in 1627 at Messing in Essex, the son of
Nehemiah Rogers, the vicar of the parish. Though Nehemiah
was a staunch royalist and supporter of Archbishop Laud—a
twofold loyalty for which he was deprived of his living in 1642
—young John, while still a schoolboy, listened eagerly to
sermons by Puritan divines, and they made a deep and lasting
impression on him. In 1637 a sermon by Dr. William Fenner, the
Puritan rector of Rochford in Essex, so startled Rogers that
he remembered passages from it for years afterwards.

One day when he was in church, he said, he heard Dr. Fenner:

Full of zeal, stirring about and thundring and beating the pulpit;
I was amazed and thought he was mad; I wondred what he meant,
and whilest I was gazing upon him I was struck, and saw it was we

---

[5] R. W. Blencowe, *Sydney Papers* (London 1825), pp. 139–41.
[6] E. Ludlow, *Memoirs* (edited C. H. Firth, Oxford 1894), Vol.
I, p. 352.

Man: w^t dost meane to gaze: Alf's but a Shade
Of th' Substance, wch the Shining Sunn hath made
The Misterie's within the Veile of Clay,
Whose Heart's ascendant in the milkie Way,
The Shadow's leafe, the Substance life. Both Show
Christ's motion's Swift, Haft: Haft: run like ye RO,

: Sauill innxit.   W: Hollar fecit 1657

JOHN ROGERS 1653

that were mad, which made him so; O sayes he! you knotty, rugged, proud piece of flesh! you stony, rocky, flinty, hard heart! what wilt thou doe when thou art roaring in Hell amongst the damned? . . .[7]

This so terrified young Rogers, aged ten, that from then on-wards, through fear of hell-fire, he listened to as many sermons as he could, and read the Scriptures assiduously morning and night. Moreover he took notes of the sermons, memorized them, and repeated one sermon aloud each night just before he went to bed. Soon he found that he had so many prayers and other pieces to say each night during his self-imposed ritual that, so he re-corded later, 'You must know, having so much to do every night, I sometimes began (to myself whilst I sate in the chimney-corner) before supper, and usually left nothing but my sermon to repeat for my bed. . . .'[7]

He was so frightened of going to Hell that he made a practice of going to sleep with his hands clasped in prayer, believing that if he died in his sleep this holy posture would safeguard him from all harm. Even during the day-time, however, he was not free from his terrors. 'Every thunder and lightning I look'd upon as my fate, and sent for me; and then would I fall to my prayers and saying my creed and commandments and my sermons as fast as might be. . . .'[7]

It is not surprising that a boy who subjected himself to such a morbid way of life should show signs of mental unbalance; and in fact young Rogers had what he later described as 'raging fits' from time to time. The treatment which he received for these was primitive in the extreme, and not calculated to cure his disorder. To quote his own words once more, he was 'taken and bound hand and foot, and held or tied fast in a bed till the raging fits were over'.[7]

These 'raging fits' were trial enough to Nehemiah; but when his son began to associate more and more with extreme Puritans, the outrage felt by the devout Anglican prevailed over the feel-ings of a father, and so John, in 1642, was turned away from home. He tried to enter Cambridge as a student, but failed; and then began a dreary existence of near-starvation when he was reduced to trying to eat grass to keep alive. From this, however,

---

[7] J. Rogers, *Ohel or Bethshemesh* (1653), Book II, Chapter 6.

he was rescued by the offer of a teaching post in Huntingdonshire. That very night he had a strange dream, in which 'a
grave ancient man full of white hairs like wool' declared that he
had been sent by God to inform Rogers that he had been chosen
to preach the Gospel of Christ.

Fortified by this revelation, Rogers began to preach in Huntingdonshire, and made such an impression that in 1647 he was
able to return to his native Essex as Presbyterian minister of
Purleigh. While in Huntingdonshire, however, he had come into
close contact with the uncompromising Parliamentarians of the
Eastern Association commanded by Cromwell, and this appears
to have given him a taste for politics which he could not indulge
in the rural seclusion of Purleigh.

He therefore arranged for a curate to look after the parish, and
departed for London. Here he dropped his Presbyterian doctrines, became an Independent, and accepted a lectureship[8] at the
church of St. Thomas Apostle (destroyed in the Great Fire of
London and not rebuilt) in Vintry Ward of the City, on the
west side of Queen Street. His political sermons attracted such
favourable notice that he was despatched by Parliament to
preach in Dublin, where he remained for two years (1650–2).
When he returned, in April 1652, the differences of opinion between the Army and Parliament were becoming more and more
bitter; and Rogers, who had now become a convinced Fifth
Monarchy Man, joined vigorously in the political controversies
of the day.

He supported the cause of the Army, because it was the
cause of the Independents, and because the Army numbered in
its ranks a number of Fifth Monarchy Men, such as Major-
General Harrison and Colonel Rich. Rogers knew that the day
after Cromwell had turned out the Rump a meeting of the leading army officers had been called to consider what new kind of
government should be set up; and Rogers accordingly went
eagerly to work compiling a series of proposals which, if adopted,
would inaugurate the rule of the saints. His proposals, submitted
on 25 April 1653, were headed: 'To His Excellency the Lord

---

[8] Lecturers were preachers, usually clergymen without a benefice, who were specially engaged to preach, and whose lectures
were, in fact, sermons.

General Cromwell, A few proposals relating to Civil Government, Humbly offered by John Rogers, an unworthy servant
of Christ, and preacher of the Gospel, now at Tho. Apostles,
London.' The author began: 'Right Honourable, whilst my
soul is boyling over into earnest prayers to the great Jehovah
for Wisdome, Counsel and Courage for you in this Exigency
of importance, as the great Deliverer of his people (through
God's grace) out of the house of Egypt...' He went on to
say that after a solemn prayer-meeting with hundreds of people
at St. Thomas Apostle's, he would like to submit certain proposals. First, Cromwell himself should choose the new men
who were to govern the Commonwealth. Secondly, there should
be a Parliament or 'Synedrin' (i.e. Sanhedrim—the highest
court and supreme council in ancient Jerusalem) of seventy
members. Thirdly, these must be 'men fearing God', 'Lovers
of Truth and Justice', 'hating bribes and covetousnesse', and
possessing a number of other qualities which Rogers cited at
length, giving a biblical reference for each.

Fundamentally, Rogers' proposals were not very different
from others which were being put forward by some members of
the Council of Officers which Cromwell had called together.
Major-General Harrison, for example, was in favour of a
Sanhedrim; Colonel Okey, another Fifth Monarchist, though
also in favour of limiting the new Government to men selected
for their godliness, wanted a more restricted body than a Sanhedrim of seventy members. He wished the supreme Council to
consist of only thirteen members, a number representing Christ
and the twelve apostles. Okey, like Harrison, had made a success-
ful military career for himself during the Civil War, though when
it began he was employed in the very humble capacity of dray-
man in an Islington brewery. Again like Harrison, Okey had sat as
a member of the court which tried and condemned King
Charles; and his radical and religious sentiments made him a
willing convert to the doctrines of the Fifth Monarchy Men.

After lengthy deliberations during which all proposals were
carefully considered, the Council of Officers came to a series of
decisions on the new form of government which gave great satisfaction to Rogers, Harrison, Okey and other Fifth Monarchy
Men who wanted England to be ruled by the saints. It was
agreed that as an executive there should be a Council of State,

to consist of Cromwell and twelve others (eight army officers and four civilians). As for a legislature, the congregations of the Independent churches throughout the country were to nominate persons 'faithful, fearing God, and hating covetousness' for consideration by Cromwell and his officers. From the nominees 140 were to be chosen to sit as a parliamentary assembly.

The Council of State met for the first time on 29 April 1653; and while preparations for the convening of the assembly were going forward the indefatigable John Rogers was busy offering further advice to Cromwell and his officers. In May 1653 Rogers submitted new suggestions to 'The Right Honourable his Excellencie The Lord General Cromwel', which he prefaced with the following words:

My Lord, you never need prayers more than now, and amongst other things to protect you from Parasites serene (whilest Syrene) songs; for when the wind sings and whistles in the leaves we look for a storm, Spiders will be working in great men's pallaces, and waspes swarm in the warmest places, and so will flatterers, I am sure.

After mentioning the proposals he had made on 25 April, Rogers added some further guiding principles for Cromwell to observe in establishing the new regime. Persons who held the most responsible positions should be chosen for one year only— for, so Rogers observed, 'running waters are alwaies sweetest'. The new Government must free the people from the oppressions practised by lawyers, from tithes, from the 'soul-tyrannizing' system of presentation to livings, and from all the rest of 'Parish Church Constitutions'. On the other hand, the Independent and Congregational Churches should be cherished and nourished— for they only were 'the Gates and Pallaces of Sion'.

Rogers declared that there were a 'hidden number of Saints', and said that Cromwell must be a shield to these against their enemies. Those saints were as yet little known; but they would soon be heard of, 'when the Elements are a little clearer'. Rogers concluded his exhortations to Cromwell with the following words: 'For these ends and uses the Lord our God (we trust) hath anointed and appointed you; wherefore let these lines be accepted by your Excellency, and serve for refreshment to you in your subscisive [i.e. leisure] hours. . . .'

In a second prefatory epistle, this time to Lieutenant-General Fleetwood, Commander of the forces in Ireland, he wrote: 'I need not tell you that all the teetering and tumbling affairs on Earth now (which is universally shaking into a new Creation) are an History of Christ's coming to reign. . . .'

This conviction that the millennium was very near at hand was shared by John Spittlehouse, another Fifth Monarchy pamphleteer, who unlike John Rogers had actually served in the parliamentary army during the Civil War. Impressed by the momentous significance of the change of government which had been decided upon, Spittlehouse decided that Cromwell should have the benefit of his advice also. This was contained in a tract published on 5 July 1653, under the following title:

The First
Addresses
to
His Excellencie the Lord General
with the Assembly of Elders
elected by him and his Council for the management
of the affairs of this Commonwealth;
As also, to all the cordial Officers and Souldiers under his
command,
containing
Certain Rules and Directions
How to advance the Kingdom of Jesus
Christ over the face of the whole earth.
By John Spittlehouse, a late Member of the Army, and a
servant to the Saints of the most high God. . . .

In his preface Spittlehouse said that Cromwell, and the assembly, had been called by God 'to destroy Antichrist in his Dragonical and Priestly power, with their appendancies, and to advance the Kingdom of Jesus Christ'. Cromwell, however, was not to rest content with doing this at home; he must 'persevere in the work of the Lord in forraign parts, and not make peace with the Gibeonites or any other Nation which the Lord hath a controverse withal, and who are designed to destruction'.

It was to be hoped, in fact, that the Lord would lead Cromwell over Jordan into the land of the Canaanites, that was, over the Narrow Seas into Holland and France and to Rome itself, so that he could pluck out all the antichristian Powers who opposed Jesus Christ. The Elders of the Assembly would not, Spittlehouse hoped, be ignorant of the reason why they had been called to their high office. It was to accomplish the grand design of their Lord and Master Jesus Christ 'in these overturning, overturning, overturning days'. The design was the extension of Christ's Kingdom 'to the uttermost parts of the earth', till the saints of the most high God had taken the dominion and greatness of the Kingdom under the whole heaven into their possession.

Gentlemen, [Spittlehouse continued] if these be your intentions, then ride on and prosper; but if otherwise, then sudden destruction shall come upon you unawares, as it did upon your late predecessors; but I hope better things of you, though I thus speak: but nevertheless, inasmuch as the Lord hath been pleased to call out this our Nation as a theater to act as a president [sic] of what he intends to do in all the Nations under the cope of heaven, it behoveth you therefore, before you set yourselves in the seat of judicature, in relation to other nations, to begin at home. . . . Therefore I beseech you . . . be not like your predecessors, with a heart and a heart, one for Christ, and another for Antichrist; with a heart to abolish Prelacie, and not Presbytery; to take away Bishops, Deans and Chapters, lands etc. and yet to retain Presbytery and their tythes. For be you well assured that if you halt (as did your predecessors) betwixt light and darkness, Christ and Antichrist, God and Mammon, like the lukewarm Laodicean, . . . the Lord will as well spue you out, as he did your predecessors, of whom it is reported, that they were Sermon-proof.

Spittlehouse, Rogers, and the rest of the Fifth Monarchy Men were quite convinced that the long-awaited inauguration of the rule of the saints was now at hand. They were equally convinced that the instrument to bring about the glorious consummation was the assembly of 140 elders, or men 'faithful, fearing God and hating covetousness' chosen by the Independent church congregations, the 'Pallaces of Sion'. These men were soon to meet to begin their great work; and to this happy event Rogers, Spittlehouse, Harrison, and their friends and followers looked forward with triumphant expectation.

3

SAINTS REJECTED

THE assembly to which the Fifth Monarchy Men looked forward with so much enthusiasm sat for the first time on 4 July 1653. The members were summoned to the Council Chamber in Whitehall to hear an address by Cromwell; and from the fervent, almost ecstatic words which he used, it was clear that he too, unless he was a master-dissembler, thought that the country was on the verge of a new auspicious era. After describing recent events Cromwell proceeded to 'lay a charge' on the assembly.

Truly you are called by God [he said] to rule with Him, and for Him. And you are called to be faithful with the Saints, who have been somewhat instrumental to your call. . . . I confess I never looked to see such a day as this—it may be, nor you neither—when Jesus Christ should be so owned as He is, at this day, and in this work.[1]

Many men in England shared Cromwell's hope and belief, though not, as it turned out, for precisely the same reasons. The Civil War had resulted in the overthrow of the monarchy and the establishment of a Commonwealth; but revolutions have a habit of gaining momentum, and what would nowadays be called a left-wing developed in England, a group who wished to continue the revolutionary reforming impulse into the sphere of social and economic affairs. Prominent among these left-wing reformers were the Levellers, and after their eclipse, the Fifth Monarchy Men.

It must be conceded that in many respects the calls for reform were justified. The legal system, for example, suffered from many abuses, including venality, anachronistic survivals of the feudal system, and unconscionable delays, and in such circumstances when the poor were at a manifest disadvantage, there was no real equality before the law. Other features of the legal system,

---

[1] Abbot, *The Writings and Speeches of O. Cromwell* (Cambridge, Mass. 1937–47), Vol. III, pp. 61–63.

such as excessively harsh and cruel punishments, and self-defeating measures such as imprisonment for debt, also raised calls for reform.

Similarly, in the ecclesiastical sphere, tithes still pressed heavily and unfairly on many people, often on persons who objected on grounds of conscience to paying them to lay impropriators, or to contributing to maintain a church system which they thought wrong, or even ungodly. Advowsons, the right to present to livings, came under criticism for the same reasons.

In the economic affairs of the nation the system of taxation and revenue raising was the subject of many attacks. Arbitrary assessment in general was complained of; and customs dues and the seventeenth-century innovation, the excise, were held to press particularly heavily and unfairly on the mass of the people because their effect was to raise the price of goods.

When the long-awaited assembly of the men 'called by God' began its session on 4 July, therefore, it could be said that it had work enough to do if it was minded to make of England the new Jerusalem.

This was indeed a time of exultation and glory for the saints, and books and pamphlets were published in confident expectation that the beginning of Christ's Kingdom was very close at hand. The Fifth Monarchist William Aspinwall was especially active. In March 1653 he had published: 'An Explication and Application of the Seventh Chapter of Daniel'. In this Aspinwall traced the downfall of the four monarchies, and examined the history of the ten horns or kingdoms which had developed after the fall of the Roman Empire. He sought to prove that Charles I was the Little Horn, and in a preface addressed to Cromwell he acknowledged that God had chosen the Lord General to be a 'choice instrument' to execute the biblical judgement on the Little Horn. Nevertheless, Aspinwall said, much still remained to be done. The Beast, it was true, had been slain; but the evil features of the old regime had not been eradicated. Therefore, in the words of David (1 Chron. xxii. 16), Cromwell must arise and be doing; and the Lord would then be with him.

On 1 August 1653, while the new assembly was still in undisturbed session, and the saints' tenure of power seemed secure, Aspinwall published a second work which reflected the confidence with which the Fifth Monarchy Men were imbued at this time. The new work was entitled:

A Brief Description
of the
Fifth Monarchy,
or
Kingdome,
That shortly is to come into the World.

In it Aspinwall denied that the texts (Daniel, etc.) upon which he based his expectations were, as unbelievers said, to be interpreted metaphorically. It was not safe 'to coin metaphors of Scripture', Aspinwall declared, and he maintained that the prophecies of Daniel and the other seers must be read literally, according to 'the plaine meaning of the words'. Aspinwall concluded that 'the uttermost durance of Antichrist's dominion will be in the year 1673, as I have proved from Scripture in a brief chronology ready to be put forth'; but—he added prudently, 'as for the precise yeare, I dare not determine'.

John Rogers was a prominent protagonist of the radical reforms which the Fifth Monarchy Men wanted, especially with regard to the law and the Church; but though his detestation of lawyers and churchmen was undoubtedly based on a deep dislike of current abuses, an element of personal hostility also contributed to the rancorous diatribes which he spread abroad. For example, his flock at Purleigh in Essex, not unnaturally dissatisfied with an absentee pastor, succeeded in getting him relieved of his duties because of his non-residence. Rogers never forgave them. He told them that his greatest grief for most of them was, that like the cypress, the more they were watered the more they withered; and this anger directed against the Presbyterians of Purleigh he transferred to Presbyterians at large.

Similarly, the legal suit in which he became involved over the issue of non-residence at Purleigh brought Rogers into personal contact with lawyers and the legal procedures of the day; and he ascribed his defeat in the suit to the crafty machinations of rascally lawyers. Thenceforth he had nothing but savage condemnation for the English legal system in general, and for lawyers in particular.

In his book *Ohel or Bethshemesh* he set forth his ideas on

A Brief Description
OF THE
Fifth Monarchy,
OR
KINGDOME,
That shortly is to come into the World.

The Monarch, Subjects, Officers, and Lawes thereof, and the surpassing Glory, Amplitude, Unity, and Peace of that *Kingdome*.

When the Kingdome and Dominion, and the greatnesse of the Kingdome under the whole Heaven shall be given to the people, the Saints of the Most high, whose Kingdome is an everlasting Kingdome, and all Soveraignes shall serve and obey him.

And in the Conclusion *there is added a* Prognostick *of the time when this fifth Kingdome shall begin.*

By WILLIAM ASPINWALL, *N. E.*

2 Pet. 3. 13. *Neverthelesse, we according to his promise, look for New Heavens, and a new Earth, wherein dwels righteousnesse.*

Psal. 2. 10, 11, 12. *Be wise therefore O yee Kings : be instructed yee Judges of the Earth. Serve the Lord with feare, and rejoyce with trembling. Kisse the Son least he be angry, and yee perish from the way, when his wrath is kindled but a little.*

Psal. 76. 12. *For, he will cut off the Spirit of Princes ; he is terrible to the Kings of the Earth.*

Job 12. 21. *He poureth contempt upon Princes : he is terrible to the Kings of the Earth.* August y̍ 1.

LONDON:
Printed by *M. Simmons*, and are to be sold by *Livewell Chapman* at the *Crown* in *Popeshead-Alley.* 1653.

Church government, and attacked those who differed from him, particularly Anglicans and Presbyterians, with great vigour. The book, which was divided into two parts, *Dod or Chathan, The Beloved: or the Bridegroom going forth for his Bride*, and *Challah, the Heavenly Nymph: or the Bride*, was published on 7 November 1653. In it Rogers wrote laboriously and at great length to prove that the system of Church government by independent congregations or 'gathered churches' was the only one sanctioned by Scripture. He poured forth all his invective on the Anglican and Presbyterian systems, which were hierarchical and based on parishes; and the index which he considerately provided for his readers abounds with entries such as:

Beasts meet together in parish churches. . . .
Captivity of Babylon in parish churches, bondage. . . .
Impudent whoredoms of parish churches, ministers and people. . . .

In another publication, which also appeared on 7 November 1653, Rogers explained what was wrong with the existing legal system in England. The resounding and intimidating title of this work was:

Sagrir,
or
Doomes-day drawing nigh,
With Thunder and Lightening to Lawyers,
In an Alarum
For New Laws, and the Peoples Liberties from the
Norman and Babylonian Yokes.

Rogers addressed his preface to 'The Right Honourable the Lord Gen. Cromwell, the Peoples Victorious Champion in England, Ireland and Scotland'. He declared that the eyes of thousands were upon the Lord General, to see what he would do to restore the liberty and freedom which Englishmen had lost as a result of the Norman conquest and tyranny. 'It is far better for us, my Lord,' Rogers continued, 'now to hang us, then [sic] not to help us against the insufferable Laws and Lawyers, which rob us of Justice and righteousnesse!'

Cromwell, he said, must hearken unto the cries of the people 'for justice upon the usurping proud Lawyers, for their lying, perjury and treachery'; and he pursued the theme relentlessly in a second preface, addressed to his readers in general. He

סַגְרִיר *Sagrir.*

OR

Doomes-day drawing *nigh,*

With Thunder and Lightening to L A W Y E R S.

In an *Alarum*
For *New Laws,* and the *Peoples Liberties* from the
Norman and *Babylonian* Yokes.

Making Difcoverie
Of the *prefent* ungodly *Laws* and *Lawyers* of the *Fourth Monarchy,*
and of the approach of the *F I F T H*; with thofe godly *Laws,*
Officers and *Ordinances* that belong to the *Legiflative Power* of the Lord *Iefus.*

SHEWING

The *Glorious Work* Incumbent to *Civil-Difcipline,* (once more) fet
before the *Parliament,* Lord *Generall, Army* and *People* of *England,* in
their diftinct *capacities,* upon the *Accoxnt* of *Chrift* and his *Monarchy.*

Humbly prefented to them by J O H N R O G E R S, *an unfained* Servant
of Chrift, *and this* Common-wealth *in their beft* Rights, Laws
and Liberties, loft many years.

Bread of Deceit is fweet to a man, but afterwards his mouth fhall be filled with Gravell.
Prov. 20.17.
Whofo ftoppeth his ears at the cry of the poor, he fhal cry himfelf, but fhal not be heard.
Prov. 21.13.
They are Braffe and Iron, they are all Corrupters, the Bellows are burnt, the Lead is con-
fumed of the fire, the Founder melteth in vain, for the Wicked are not plucked a-
way. *Ier.* 6. 28. 29.

נִשְׁמְטוּ פִירֵי־סֶלַע שָׁפְטֵיהֶם וְשָׁמְעוּ אֲמָרַי כִּי נָעֵמוּ When

their Judges (or the greateft *Lawyers*) are thrown down into ftony places, they fhall
hear my *Words,* becaufe then they are fweet, *Pfal.* 141. 6.

Caufidicis, Erebo, Fifco, *fas vivere rapto;*
Militibus, Medico, Tortori, *occidere ludo;*
Mentiri Aftrologis, Pictoribus, atque Poetis.

Nou. 9.

L O N D O N,
Printed by R. I. to be fold by *Giles Calvert* at the *Black-fpread Eagle,* at
the *Weft* end of *Pauls.* 1654. 1653

proclaimed that these had work to do 'about the Lawes and
Tithes, to strip the whore both of her outward scarlet array, and
to rend the flesh off her bones, by throwing down the standing
of Lawyers and Priests'. In short, the citizens of the 'Commonwealth of England' had to prepare for the Fifth Monarchy by
introducing the laws of God.

The first chapter of Rogers' book was entitled 'How the
Lawyers are Antichrists State-Army of Locusts', and he went on
to describe them as 'the corrupt, cruel, oppressing, cursed brew
of lawyers', who were 'as wicked a generation of cheates and
tyrants as the Earth bears'. In subsequent chapters, copiously
larded with similar abuse, Rogers explained that the people of
England had lived freely under 'plain honest law' until the
Norman Conquest. After this 'William the Tyrant' had subjected
them to oppressive unjust laws constituting a bondage from
which they had never been able afterwards to free themselves.
Englishmen, Rogers said, whether they were religious or not, all
cried aloud for deliverance from the Norman yoke; and it was
chiefly because of this that the people's eyes and cries were
directed to the Lord General.

Rogers next turned to a consideration of the Fifth Monarchy.
'That there is such a kingdom to come', he asserted, 'is
obvious to all intelligent men, by abundance of Scriptures'; and
he proceeded to cite copiously from Daniel and Revelation to
prove this statement. 'Though men be of divers minds as to the
precise time', he continued, 'yet all concur in the nighnesse and
swiftnesse of its coming upon us.'

As far as the Little Horn was concerned, Rogers was convinced that by it was meant the entire line of 'Norman' kings
stretching from William the Conqueror to Charles I, and that
the execution of the latter in 1649 signified the end of the
Little Horn as foretold in Daniel (xii. 7). The other ten horns
were the kingdoms of Europe, such as France, Spain, and Den-
mark, and though these would have a brief respite after the
Little Horn had been 'cut off', the Fifth Monarchy would soon
infallibly be ushered in, and their doom would be sealed. 'Within this seaven yeares', Rogers confidently asserted, 'by one
thousand six hundred and sixty, the worke will get as farre as
Rome, and by one thousand six hundred and sixty six this
Monarchy must be visible in all the Earth!'

The Fifth Monarchy would come mysteriously, but suddenly; and when it came it would redeem the people of England from their ecclesiastical and legal bondage, for, Rogers exulted, 'The whore shall be striped stark naked, and made desolate', and Englishmen would be rescued from 'those bloody, base, unjust, accursed, tyrannical laws, and sin-monopolizing lawyers, as now oppresse and afflict the people.... Woe to the lawyers and Priests!' It followed that 'all the laws and ordinances, civill and ecclesiastick, of the Fourth Monarchy must tumble at the entrance of the Fifth'; and, in fact, at the end of *Sagrir* Rogers stated explicitly that because of the imminence of the Fifth Monarchy, Parliament must 'model and conforme the civil affaires for Christ's coming'.

The assembly which had met for the first time on 4 July 1653 seemed to Rogers and other Fifth Monarchy Men eminently suited, because of the way in which it had been chosen, to carry out the wholesale spring-cleaning operation which they thought was called for to prepare for Christ's coming. Nevertheless, the assembly from which so much was fondly hoped came to be called derisively 'Barebone's Parliament', from Praise-God Barbon, a leather-seller of Fleet Street, who was one of its more prominent members; and the disrepute into which it fell was succinctly summed up by the Earl of Clarendon in his *History of the Rebellion and Civil Wars in England*. 'In a word,' he wrote, 'they [i.e. the members of the assembly] were a pack of weak, senseless fellows, fit only to bring the name and reputation of Parliament lower than it was yet.'[2]

Clarendon's strictures were not wholly deserved, however. For one thing, the assembly contained many men of rank, substance, and influence, such as baronets, knights, high-ranking officers, and Justices of the Peace, who certainly did not deserve the contemptuous description 'weak and senseless fellows', as events were to show. The members proved, in fact, to be earnest, hard-working, and in many cases practical men; and some of the reforms which they made, or tried to make, reflected an enlightened spirit in advance of the age, and were an anticipation of the work of the nineteenth century.

---

[2] *History of the Rebellion and Civil Wars in England* (Oxford 1888), Vol. V, p. 282.

During their five months' session the members strove hard to fulfil the hopes, shared by many others in addition to the Fifth Monarchy Men, that a thoroughgoing reform would be made at last of the existing legal, financial, and ecclesiastical systems, and that a greater measure of social justice would be introduced into the land. In particular, the vigour with which the assembly began its work greatly encouraged the advocates of reform.

On 5 July 1653 the members took up their quarters in the old House of Commons, and one of their first decisions was to co-opt Cromwell, Major-General Harrison, and three other officers. Committees were appointed to consider such pressing problems as reform of the law, and the condition of the poor, and then, on 15 July, a frontal attack was made on the problem of tithes. It was proposed that no tithes should be paid as maintenance for ministers after 3 November 1653; but this was not taken to a division, and instead, by a narrow majority of fifty-six votes to forty-nine, the problem of tithes was referred to committee.

The discussion and controversy about tithes had revealed a division in the assembly between radical and more conservatively-minded reformers, and this was to become more and more apparent as the days went by. The advocates of thoroughgoing reform, who had supported the proposal concerning tithes, con-stituted a minority of the assembly, and among them were the Fifth Monarchist members, though these numbered less than twenty. Prominent among them was Major-General Harrison, however, and what they lacked in numbers they made up for in enthusiasm and initiative, particularly in committee work. They met often at the house of a prominent Fifth Monarchy Man named Squibb, and there, and at meetings with Christopher Feake and his congregation in Blackfriars, they conceived and elaborated the proposals which they later brought forward in Barebone's Parliament.

On 5 August a major proposal was brought forward in the assembly, concerning the Court of Chancery. The unpopularity of that institution was reflected in the fact that after a single day's debate a majority of the House agreed that the court should be abolished, and requested the law committee to draft a bill providing for this. On 19 August the problem of codification of the law was referred to committee, in order that in future the laws of the land should be 'easy, plain and short'. On 24 August a majority of the House again reached agreement and passed an Act establishing civil marriage solemnized by Justices of the Peace, and providing also for uniform registration of births, marriages, and deaths. Other Acts which were passed without undue controversy provided for the relief of poor prisoners and lunatics; and the assembly, despite the division of opinion within it, seemed to be on the way towards achieving some, at least, of the great work expected from it.

However, the fears of the moderates were reawakened when on 17 November, by fifty-eight votes to forty-one, the House approved a proposal to abolish the right of lay presentation to livings, and when, on 2 December, a report of the committee on tithes was submitted for consideration. This recommended *inter alia* that State Commissioners should travel round England on circuit, ejecting ministers found unfit or unqualified, and replacing them with others deemed to be more suitable. This proposal generated great controversy, and on 10 December it was finally defeated by the narrow majority of fifty-six votes to fifty-four.

The moderates were now convinced that Major-General Harrison and his supporters intended to stop at nothing until they had effected a radical transformation of England in accordance with Fifth Monarchist principles; and to prevent further troubles they decided to put an end to the assembly by resigning its powers into the hands of Cromwell. By arrangement they met early in the morning of Monday, 12 December, when some of the radicals had not yet arrived, and Sir Charles Wolseley made himself the spokesman.

He condemned the policies of the radicals, said he would be no party to them, and then proposed that the members of the assembly should return to Cromwell the powers which they had received a few months before. Those radicals who were present objected to the proposal, but their objections were rejected. Finally, the Speaker rose from his chair, and followed by some forty members he left the chamber for Whitehall, where the powers of the assembly were duly resigned into Cromwell's hands.

Major-General Harrison and some twenty-seven other members of the Parliament had dissented strongly from these proceedings, and after the Speaker and the moderates had left the chamber, remained obstinately seated in their places, till they were ignominiously turned out by a detachment of musketeers. As he departed Harrison must surely have remembered the last occasion when members of Parliament had been unceremoniously bundled out of their House: that had been in April 1653, but in different circumstances. Then, Harrison had been one of the agents of the expulsion. Now he was one of the victims!

It has been said that the premature end of Barebone's Parliament was due to the antagonism it aroused among vested interests—lawyers, lay-impropriators of tithes, landlords, and so on—who saw their position and privileges threatened. There is, of course, a great deal of truth in this; but it is not the whole truth. The conservatively-minded moderates were not merely doubtful about some of the more drastic changes which the radicals had already proposed. They were also apprehensive of what, if they were not restrained, the minority would try to get passed into law in the future.

In view of the fact that Harrison and his colleagues were ardent disciples of Fifth Monarchy doctrines as expounded by such uncompromising exponents of the faith as Rogers and Feake, the apprehensions of the moderates in Barebone's Parliament can hardly be said to have been ill-founded. They feared, not without cause, that if the radical minority had their way it would lead, not to the reform, but to the overthrow of existing laws and institutions, without due provision having been made beforehand for a practical working system in their place, and thus, in short, to chaos.

As it happened, the radical minority were not allowed to have their way, and so it is impossible to say dogmatically that the fears and accusations of the moderates were justified. In the existing circumstances, however, it was fully understandable that those fears were expressed, and that appropriate counter-measures were taken.

The end of Barebone's Parliament meant that Cromwell and the Army leaders were again faced with the problem of devising a new form of government; and after much earnest debate the Council of Officers decided on a new constitution which was embodied in a document called 'The Instrument of Government'. Under this the country was to become a Protectorate, with Cromwell as Lord Protector, assisted by a small council of persons appointed for life, whilst the legislative power was to be exercised by a Parliament representing England, Scotland, Ireland and Wales, elected in accordance with provisions which made changes in the distribution of constituencies and the franchise. The new Parliament was to meet on 3 September 1654, and until then the Protector, with the approval of his council, was empowered to make ordinances having the power of laws.

Rogers, Harrison, and the other Fifth Monarchy Men were bitterly disappointed over the untimely end of the Parliament of God-fearing men which had dispersed before completing its work of preparing England for the rule of the saints. They consequently regarded the new constitution with the utmost dislike and suspicion, and were not slow to voice their feeling. On 21 December 1653, five days after the decision to establish the Protectorate, John Rogers addressed a number of 'humble cautionary proposals' to Cromwell, which clearly reflected deep distrust of the future trend of events.

First, Rogers said, the Lord Protector was to take heed of protecting the plantations of Antichrist, or the towers of Babylon. Secondly, he must beware of 'carnal counsellors' who would tempt him to be guided by 'old-State principles' of carnal policy, instead of the righteous precepts expounded by the godly men, the saints, of the commonwealth. Rogers enlarged on this by recurring to his favourite themes. He warned Cromwell not to protect 'men's carnal, cruel, heathenish lawes . . . most of them contrary to the laws of God'; and he was equally to take heed of protecting 'the carnal, national, antichristian clergy' who by flattery would seek to seduce Cromwell into the cause of Antichrist.

Rogers ended his 'humble cautionary proposals' with a stern warning:

If you will freely oblige for Christ and his interest, the faith and prayers of the Saints (which were never higher than now) shall protect you sufficiently in all emergencies; but if you will ingage for Antichrist and his Interest, the loud-crying Faith and incessant high-spirited Prayers of the Saints will all ingage against you. . . . Take heed what you do!

However, some of the saints were not prepared merely to wait on events, to see whether the Lord Protector, by his future actions, should merit their condemnation. They rejected him utterly now, as the person in their eyes most responsible for the overthrow of the late Parliament, as the perfidious betrayer of the cause of the godly, and as the chief obstacle to the inauguration of the reign of King Jesus and his saints.

Christopher Feake was one of the most loquacious and virulent of these disappointed Fifth Monarchy Men. The date of his birth and other details of his early life are unknown; but during the Civil War he became prominent as an Independent minister in London, and as a 'lecturer' at St. Anne's, Blackfriars, Allhallows the Great in Upper Thames Street, and other City churches. In 1649 he became vicar of Christ Church, Newgate Street,[3] and about this time too his beliefs, which had always been unconventional and verging on the eccentric, became definitely transmuted into Fifth Monarchy doctrines. According to his own account, the first meeting of the Fifth Monarchy Men at Allhallows occurred in December 1651,[4] and soon the sect became a close-knit little community in the City of London and its environs. Feake's own Fifth Monarchy fanaticism grew with the years, and when Barebone's Parliament, an assembly on which he had set great hopes, was prematurely ended, his disappointment and fury were both unbounded. He regarded Cromwell as primarily responsible for the disastrous turn which events had taken, and scourged him verbally for what he considered his disgraceful apostasy.

Equally virulent was Vavasor Powell, a Welshman born in Radnorshire in 1617, who adopted the life of an itinerant evangelist at the age of twenty-two, and who during the Civil War served not only as a chaplain, but also as a captain commanding a troop of horse under Colonel Harrison. The latter espied in him a man after his own heart—a representative of the church militant; and Powell also appealed to him because,

---

[3] St. Anne's, Blackfriars was burnt down in the Great Fire of London and not rebuilt. Allhallows the Great in Upper Thames Street was burnt down in the Great Fire, rebuilt in 1683, and demolished in the late nineteenth century during the widening of Upper Thames Street. Christ Church, Newgate Street, destroyed in the Great Fire, was rebuilt, but again suffered great damage in the Second World War.

[4] C. Feake, *A Beam of Light* (1659), p. 34.

although nominally a Baptist, he developed strong Fifth Monarchist leanings.

On Sunday, 18 December, whilst preaching at Christ Church,
Newgate Street, both Feake and Powell called Cromwell 'the
dissemblingest perjured villain in the world', and added defiantly
that if any of his friends were present in church they could go
and tell him what had been said about him. His reign in any
case, they added, would be short; and they prophesied that he
would in the end fare worse even than 'that great tyrant the
last lord protector' [i.e. King Charles] had done.

On Monday, 19 December, in accordance with ancient custom, heralds in the City and Westminster proclaimed Cromwell
Lord Protector, and this ceremony roused Feake and Powell to a
fresh outburst of fury. In the evening of the same day, at St.
Anne's, Blackfriars, Feake, who preached first, discoursed on
one of his favourite themes, the Little Horn. He showed how
Scripture revealed that this Little Horn would set himself against
the saints, and would even 'wear them out for some short time'.
However, this period of travail would be ended by the inauguration of the Fifth Monarchy, when the faithful saints would
enjoy the Kingdom and the dominion.

Feake went on to remark that he knew that some people
identified the late King Charles with the 'Little Horn'; but
from what the preacher said subsequently it was apparent that
he thought this a wrong interpretation. 'I'll name nobody,' Feake
declared, but added, 'God will make it clear shortly to his people
who is meant here!' The inference was obvious—Cromwell,
and not King Charles, was the Little Horn.

Powell followed Feake into the pulpit, and was much more
pointed than the latter in his references to Cromwell—though
Powell, too, at first named no names. A vile person, he said,
(quoting Daniel xi. 21)[5] would obtain the kingdom by flatteries:
but the people who knew their God would 'be strong and do
exploits', for Christ was even now setting up the Fifth Monarchy,
and the present power was doomed to fall.

Towards the end of his sermon Powell turned his wrath against

---

[5] 'And in his estate shall stand up a vile person, to whom they
shall not give the honour of the kingdom; but he shall come in
peaceably, and obtain the kingdom by flatteries.'

the Army officers because of their support of Cromwell: 'Lord!'
he cried out, 'have our army men all apostasized from their
principles? What is become of all their declarations, protestations
and professions? Are they choked with parks, lands and manors?
Let us go home and pray, and say, Lord, wilt thou have Oliver
Cromwell or Jesus Christ to reign over us?' Anticipating persecution, Powell observed that the saints might well be stopped soon
from meeting at St. Anne's, Blackfriars, their accustomed place
of worship. 'But then', he asserted militantly, 'we can meet
at another, and if we be driven from thence, we will meet
at private houses, and if we cannot have liberty there, we will
into the fields, and if we be driven thence, we will into corners, for
we will never give over!'[6]

Such outspoken defiance was too much for Cromwell, tolerant
though he was; and on 21 December Feake and Powell were
taken into custody. They were released, however, on 24 December,
with a caution to be of good behaviour in the future. At the
same time Harrison, because of his connexion with the Fifth
Monarchy Men, was asked whether he was prepared to support
the new regime; and when he said he was not, he was deprived
of his army commission.

As for Feake and Powell, the caution administered to them
by the Council of State had absolutely no effect. They continued to attack the Government violently in sermons at Christ
Church, Newgate Street, and on 19 January 1654, in an effort
to curb them and other enemies of the Protectorate, an ordinance was issued making it a treasonable offence to write, print,
teach, or preach that the Protector's authority was tyrannical,
usurped, or unlawful.

Under this ordinance Feake and John Simpson, Minister of
St. Botolph's, Bishopsgate, another noted Fifth Monarchy
preacher, were arrested by order of the Council of State and on
28 January imprisoned in Windsor Castle 'in order to the pre-
servation of the peace of this nation'. Previously, on 10 January,
a warrant had also been issued for the apprehension of Vavasor
Powell for preaching inflammatory sermons at Christ Church;
but for the moment he avoided arrest, having fled to the
mountains of his native Wales.

---

[6] *Calendar of State Papers Domestic* (1653–4), 20 Dec. 1653.

However, the other firebrand, John Rogers, was left at liberty
by the authorities; and at St. Thomas Apostle's he continued to
preach the cause of the saints, though somewhat more circum-
spectly than his imprisoned brethren had done. In February 1654
he was suspected of being involved in a plot against the Government to which Major-General Harrison was also said, by a
Government informant, to be a party. As a result of the denuncia-
tion Harrison was ordered to retire to his home at Newcastle-
under-Lyme; but once again, for some reason or another, Rogers
was allowed to continue his subversive activities at St. Thomas
Apostle's.

On 28 March, fortified perhaps by the immunity which he
had so far enjoyed, he arranged for a special service to begin at
seven o'clock in the morning at his church 'in solemn humiliation before the Lord'. This was to protest against the manner in
which the Government had been established, and Barebone's
Parliament brought to an end, the members of the latter having
been dispersed, so Rogers said, simply because they had wanted
to govern England as saints. The service was also to be held to
protest against 'the present grand apostasy of eminent persons
from their former principles', and against the ordinance of
treason under which the faithful remnant of saints were
threatened with persecution. Finally, those at the service were to
mourn 'the present unseasonable weather and drought, which
threatens famine', and—a typical Rogers flourish—to pray to the
Lord to remove the evil causes responsible for the manifestations
of divine displeasure.

Government agents were present when the service began on
28 March, and submitted later to the authorities a lengthy report
of what Rogers had said. In some of his prayers passages such as
the following had occurred: 'Hasten the time when all absolute
power shall be devolved into the hand of Christ; when we shall
have no Lord Protector but our Lord Jesus. . . . Look in mercy
upon thy Saints at Windsor, that are imprisoned for the truth
and the testimony of Jesus!'

In other prayers Rogers was reported to have made highly un-
complimentary references to Cromwell and the Council of State,
though no names were mentioned, referring to 'their ridiculous
pomp and vanity' and to their 'crucifying of Christ Jesus in the
spirit' every day. According to the informants, Rogers had

ended his exhortations thus: 'In sum, my dear friends, you may shortly expect a new book of martyrs; the saints are worse dealt with by the powers of this age than they were by the heathens of old!'[7]

Even after evidence of this kind Rogers was not taken into custody, though on 7 April his house was searched and books and papers seized for examination. A few weeks later, still smarting under this reprisal, but still at liberty, Rogers wrote another letter to Cromwell. This was published on 10 June, under the title:

Mene, Tekel, Perez,[8]

or

A Little Appearance of the
Hand-Writing
(In a Glance of Light)
Against the Powers and Apostates of the
Times.
By a Letter written to, and lamenting over,
Oliver Lord Cromwell.

The letter began:

My Lord,
    While the souls of many of the Lords dear Servants (who sit weeping over you) are in Travel, and struggle for you in this hour of temptation, I most humbly beg (as upon my knees) for your own Soule, and Family, and for the poor afflicted Saints sake, that you will but weigh these few lines of our present lamentation in the ballance of your heart. . . .

Rogers alleged that the Protector was ensnared by the counsel of self-seeking flatterers and parasites. As for the saints, they had no malice against anybody, but were opposed to 'the sins and

---

[7] Thurloe, *State Papers* (edited T. Birch, London 1742), Vol. III, pp. 483–5. (The date given in Thurloe for the service, 28 May 1655, is a mistake; see Gardiner, *History of the Commonwealth and Protectorate* [London 1894], Vol. III, p. 114).

[8] The writing on the wall of Belshazzar's palace, which according to Daniel's interpretation, was as follows:
    Mene: God hath numbered thy kingdom and finished it.
    Tekel: Thou art weighed in the balances and found wanting.
    Peres: Thy kingdom is divided, and given to the Medes and
        Persians. (Daniel v. 26–28.)

evil of this change of government', which was indeed contrary to all former engagements by Cromwell himself against absolute rule by one person. Rogers exhorted the Protector:

Trust not flatterers as always speak smooth things to you, and prophesie deceitfully. O, hear a little the Lords own Seers! . . . And therefore let out the Lord's prisoners (whom the churches are robbed of), viz. Mr. Feake and Mr. Simpson, and that they open to you the present vision of God given them in these things! . . . But [Rogers ended] if you will yet go on . . . after all our bleeding in-treaties, and be hardned up by the dangerous counsil of your own Reason, or them about you, then my Lord our souls shall mourn in secret for you, as for one desperately lost indeed! . . .

These exhortations and admonitions did not have the desired effect. On the contrary, the Government at last took action against Rogers; for on 26 July the Council of State decided that he should be arrested, and made to answer all the charges which had been building up against him. Accordingly, on 27 July 1654 he was consigned to Lambeth Palace under the guard of Dendy, Serjeant-at-Arms to the Council of State.

Rogers might now be incarcerated; but the stream of Fifth Monarchy invective against the Government continued, for other pens went to work to defend the cause and vituperate Cromwell. One of the most notable denunciations came from John More, who on 29 July 1654 published:

A Trumpet Sounded:
Or, The Great
Mystery
of the
Two Little Horns
Unfolded,
Being as
A Candle set up in the dark Lanthorn of Daniel.

In his foreword (which was clearly addressed to Cromwell, though the Protector was not named), More wrote:

Hearken, O Great Man (or you must be bowed down) to the voice of the Lord, which he hath commanded me, a worm, me the least among the Saints, to declare unto thee, wherby (if by any means) thou mayst have thy poor distracted soul drawn forth earnestly to pray, if perhaps the Lord may spare thee, and have mercy upon thee, by chusing some other to act the bloody Tragedie of the Little Horn, Daniel vii. 8, for thou art he: vid. inclosed.

More ended his foreword compendiously:

Sir, I am

a man of sorrows.
mourning for Sion.
waiting for King Jesus.
rising up early.
speaking late.
ready to quench the thirsty Little Horn with the blood of my heart, if that would do it.
                    John More

In the 'inclosed' which Cromwell was advised to read More went into laborious detail to explain that the Little Horn mentioned in Daniel vii. 8 was not the same as the other Little Horn referred to in Daniel viii. 9. It was the former, More declared, which 'doth clearly appear to be the Governour and Government of England at this day'; and, he added,

What can the faithful godly souls of England or any other part (where this more stout Beast than his fellows must come—Dan. vii, 20) expect, but wounds and wo; but anguish, tribulation and astonishment; but sighing, sobbing, weeping, wailing, crying, imprisoning, hanging, murthering, etc?

Though More and other Fifth Monarchy writers did their best to uphold the cause, they were not of the same calibre as Feake and Rogers; and since these chief trouble-makers were now no longer at large to enflame their followers against the regime, Cromwell and his Council could look forward with some confidence to the inaugural meeting of the Parliament to be summoned under the 'Instrument of Government'. Events were soon to show, however, that the saints could be imprisoned, but not silenced; and that the Protector was now faced not only with their implacable hostility, but also with a potentially dangerous situation.

4

SAINTS DEFIANT

On 26 July 1654, the day before Rogers was committed to Lambeth Palace, another order of the Council of State had been issued, but this time of release. The person concerned was one Hannah Trapnell, a member of the congregation of John Simpson, the Fifth Monarchy preacher, and a fervent admirer of Rogers. Hannah was a visionary who frequently went into long trances, and when she emerged from them would pray for two hours at a time, and follow this with a spell of hymn-singing. These protracted devotions soon brought her to the public notice; and as she continuously attacked Cromwell, whom she unerringly identified with the Little Horn, she drew to herself the admiration of the Fifth Monarchy Men, who thought her inspired by God. Government reaction was not so favourable, however; and on 2 June 1654 the Council of State had ordered her to be sent to Bridewell, the House of Correction in Blackfriars, where she was kept till 26 July.

Hannah Trapnell's release focused attention once more on the discontent evoked by the inauguration of the Protectorate. This found expression a little later in a Declaration published by Fifth Monarchists and a number of Baptists, on 2 September 1654. In this, 150 signatories, representing 'several of the Churches of Christ and Godly People in and about the Citie of London', dilated upon the present sufferings of Christ's cause and of his saints, and attacked the leaders of the Government and the Army for deserting the principles which they had once proclaimed.

It was in such a disturbed atmosphere that the first Parliament called under the provisions of the Instrument of Government met. On 4 September the members assembled in the Painted Chamber[1] to hear the opening address by Cromwell. The Lord

---

[1] Part of the old Royal Palace of Westminster (so called from the paintings on its walls) used by the Commons for their sessions.

Protector, mindful of the melancholy circumstances which had led to the demise of Barebone's Parliament, and conscious of the mounting, bitter criticism of his authority, deemed it necessary to talk to the new assembly at some length in order to put them without delay on the right path.

He spoke at first of the conditions prevailing in the country when he had undertaken the Government, and after some references to various disturbers of the peace such as the left-wing movement of the Levellers led by John Lilburne, he turned his attention to the Fifth Monarchy Men. Despite the venom with which they had attacked him, however, Cromwell spoke of them with remarkable forbearance and understanding. There were, he said,

many honest people, whose hearts are sincere, many of them belonging to God, and that is the mistaken notion of the Fifth Monarchy. A thing pretending more spirituality than anything else. A notion I hope we all honour, want, and hope for, that Jesus Christ will have a time to set up his reign in our hearts, by subduing those corruptions and lusts and evils that are there, which reign now more in the world than, I hope, in due time they shall do. And when more fullness of the Spirit is poured forth to subdue iniquity and bring in everlasting righteousness, then will the approach of that glory be. The carnal divisions and contentions amongst Christians, so common, are not the symptoms of that Kingdom. But for men to entitle themselves, upon this principle, that they are the only men to rule Kingdoms, govern nations, and give laws to people; to determine of property and liberty and everything else, upon such a pretence as this is: truly, they had need give clear manifestations of God's presence with them, before wise men will receive or submit to their conclusions. Besides, though certainly many of these men have good meanings, as I hope in my soul they have, yet it will be the wisdom of all knowing and experienced Christians to do as Jude saith (when he had reckoned up those horrible things done upon pretences, and happily by some upon mistakes). *Of some*, says he, *have compassion, making a difference; others save with fear, pulling them out of the fire.* (Jude 22, 23.)

'I fear they will give opportunity too often for this exercise', Cromwell then ruefully remarked; and went on to declare that if it were only a matter of 'notions' the propagators of them could be left alone. The trouble was, however, that they insisted on having their notions put into practice.

When they come to such practices [Cromwell observed] as to tell us
that liberty and property are not the badges of the Kingdom of
Christ, and tell us that instead of regulating laws, laws are to be
abrogated, indeed subverted, and would perhaps bring in the
Judaical law instead of our own known laws settled amongst us—
this is worthy of every magistrate's consideration, especially where
every stone is turned to bring confusion.[2]

Cromwell's plain talk and common sense did not have the
desired effect, either on the Fifth Monarchy Men, or on the
members of Parliament. On 11 September 1654 John Spittlehouse resumed the attack on behalf of the saints, with a publication entitled: *Certain Queries propounded to the Most Serious
Consideration of those Persons now in Power*; and on 22 September a sermon by Thomas Goodwin was published:

A
Sermon
of the
Fifth Monarchy,
Proving by Invincible Arguments
That the Saints shall have a Kingdom
here on Earth,
Which is yet to come, after the Fourth
Monarchy is destroy'd by the Sword of
the Saints, the followers of the Lamb.

In the preface to Goodwin's sermon, written by someone who
styled himself anonymously 'A Servant of the Saints', reference
was made to the aspersions lately cast by the Lord Protector on
the sect, and the writer declared: 'This term Fifth Monarchy
Men being made a mark of ignominy and reproach, I thought it
my duty to communicate it [i.e. Goodwin's sermon] to thee,
Reader, that the truth may be vindicated, and the Saints com-
forted in this evil day.'

At this time, September 1654, Vavasor Powell was still at
large in Wales, where he was busy, in his evangelistic itinerant
way, stirring up the people against Cromwell's rule. The news of
Powell's activities, and other reports and rumours, caused the
Lord Protector to take a serious view of the situation. He seems

---

[2] Abbot, *The Writings and Speeches of Oliver Cromwell*, Vol.
III, pp. 437–8.

A
SERMON
OF THE
Fifth Monarchy.

Proving by Invincible ARGUMENTS,

That the Saints shall have a Kingdom here on Earth,

Which is yet to come, after the Fourth Monarchy is destroy'd by the Sword of the Saints, the followers of the LAMB.

Preached by Mr. THO. GOODWIN, on *Rev.* 5. 9, 10.

By which it will appear, that it is for the same Truth (that formerly was so much contended for) that some of the People of God suffer at this day.

Published for the Truths sake.

Prov. 24. 21.
——— *And meddle not with them that are given to change.* ꝑ 22

Printed at *London*, for *Livewel Chapman*, at the Crown in Popes-head-Alley. 1654.

to have suspected that Harrison might be ready to lead an armed revolt against him; for about 9 September he had the exile brought from Staffordshire to London; and there, in a friendly but firm interview, warned him against 'deceitful and slippery ways whose end is destruction'.

Harrison was allowed to return to Staffordshire; and the armed revolt which the Government had feared did not, in fact, take place. The war of words by the Fifth Monarchy Men against Cromwell and the Protectorate was continued, however, both in the pulpit and in print. In July 1654 John Simpson had been released from Windsor Castle, but forbidden to come within ten miles of London. However, in December he suddenly re-appeared in the City, and defied Cromwell by preaching at Allhallows the Great. Instead of re-arresting him, the Lord Protector decided to try to reason with him, and therefore sent word asking him 'as a brother and Christian' to come with three or four members of his congregation and talk about his griev-ances. Simpson's congregation agreed that he should accept the invitation, and five members accompanied him to Whitehall.

The discussions with Cromwell began at nine in the morning and continued till noon, when the Protector excused himself as he had to keep a luncheon appointment with a foreign ambassa-dor. He had previously considerately ordered 'six dishes of meat' for Simpson and his friends; but they refused this courtesy, and instead of eating they spent the lunch hour considering how they should reply to the challenge which Cromwell had left them before adjourning the talks. They had alleged that Cromwell had deserted the principles he had previously proclaimed; and he had promptly challenged them to enumerate any promises which he had broken.

When Cromwell came back at three in the afternoon his interlocutors were ready for him. They began by alleging that he had promised to abolish tithes by 3 September. Cromwell said that he was by no means sure he had given such an under-taking; but in any case, he added, he alone could not do away with tithes—and as it happened, the members of his Council were opposed to such a policy.

The next accusation was that Cromwell had sworn to main-tain the just laws of the land—yet he had imprisoned John Simpson and Christopher Feake. The Protector's reply to this

was that he had detained the two preachers out of consideration
for their safety (and this was true, for if they had been brought to
trial under the Treason Ordinance, their lives would almost certainly have been forfeited).

Simpson next asserted that Cromwell, in agreeing to government by a single person, and by governing as that single person
himself, had not only broken former vows, but also an Act of
Parliament, which made such conduct treasonable.[3] This statement incensed Cromwell. 'Well said, Simpson!' he cried out
sarcastically, 'thou art plain indeed; not only to tell me I have
broken my vowes, but that I am in plain termes a Traitor!'

He then told Simpson curtly that he stood by his decision to
undertake the Government; and so his adversaries passed on to a
fresh point. They asserted that he had promised liberty to the
saints, but that, because of the Triers, they were now 'thrust out
of all publick liberty'.[4] In reply Cromwell stated that the Triers
had been appointed to keep knaves out of the ministry, and he
gave an assurance that their powers would not be used to ex-
clude godly men.

By now Cromwell's patience was exhausted; and judging that
no good could come from further discussion, he dismissed
Simpson and his supporters, but not without a warning. He
advised them in their own best interests to behave soberly in
future; but this exhortation was heard with impatience, and
Simpson and his companions departed feeling much displeased
with Cromwell because of what they considered his casuistical
replies to their questions.

One or two of the Fifth Monarchy preachers were less militant
than Simpson, and preferred to advocate a policy of 'wait and
see'. William Aspinwall was one of these, and on 30 November
1654 he published: 'A Premonition of Sundry Sad Calamities

---

[3] A reference no doubt to an Act of 17 March 1649, which had
made it treasonable to 'promote any person to the name, stile,
dignity, power, prerogative or authority of king'.
[4] This was a reference to an ordinance of March 1654 which
provided that all ministers admitted to a benefice during the pre-
ceding year, or thereafter to be admitted, should be examined or
'tried' to see if they were suitable. Thirty-seven commissioners or
'Triers' were appointed to carry out this 'Approbation of Public
Preachers'.

Yet to Come Grounded upon an Explication of the twenty-fourth Chapter of Isaiah!'

In his preface Aspinwall referred to Christ's imminent coming to establish his kingdom, and he exhorted the faithful to 'stand, having your loins girt'; for the twenty-fourth chapter of Isaiah did 'in a speciall manner contain the sad and inexplicable calamities' which would befall the unbelieving world shortly before the end of worldly governments and the glorious advent of Christ's Kingdom. Aspinwall was at pains, however, to explain that the Fifth Monarchy Men were of a 'sweet, peaceable, quiet, calm and cool temper', and patiently bore all troubles with fortitude, and 'without any secret plots and designes'. They merely waited and prayed for the Kingdom of Christ, secure in the knowledge that it was now at hand.

Aspinwall's description of the Fifth Monarchy Men as of a 'sweet, peaceable, quiet, calm and cool temper' could hardly be applied to some of the leading exponents of the faith, notably Christopher Feake and John Rogers. Though these two had been in custody, Feake at Windsor, and Rogers at Lambeth, for some months, nevertheless they had managed during that period to make a considerable nuisance of themselves both to their gaolers and to the Government, because of their insubordinate attitude.

In October 1654 Feake's congregation had written to him and announced with regret that they could do nothing, apart from offering up prayers, to get him released. Any other positive step, they said, such as the sending of a petition to the Protector, would have involved 'owning the Powers in Being', and this would have been tantamount to bowing the knee to the image of the Beast.

Feake, pining for freedom, was constrained to reply. He declared that the present Powers had to be recognized to a limited extent, for the alternative was anarchy. It was one thing, he explained, to own them as Powers in Being, but quite another to recognize them as lawful and righteous Powers. The prophets and martyrs in all ages had owned the Powers in Being, yet at the same time they had preached and prophesied against them because of their abominations.

The contents of Feake's letter soon became public knowledge, and his enemies gleefully proclaimed that he had recanted his

principles, in an ignoble attempt to secure his release. These insinuations provoked an angry broadside from Feake which was
published on 19 December 1654. It was entitled: 'The Oppressed Close Prisoner in Windsor-Castle, His Defiance to The
Father of Lyes in the strength of The God of Truth'.

In this tract Feake referred to the lies which he said had been
circulated about him, but asserted that he still held firmly to his
principles; and this was soon, in fact, to be proved. Undeterred
by the unsatisfactory result of his interview with John Simpson,
Cromwell decided to try reasoning once again, this time with
Feake. The latter was accordingly brought from Windsor Castle
to Whitehall on 23 December, only a few days after the appearance in print of his broadside. Cromwell allowed Feake to be
supported by some members of his congregation, but once again
the discussions proved profitless, and Feake was sent back to
Windsor Castle.

Cromwell's decision to keep Feake in confinement was probably due to fresh rumours of an impending military revolt against
his regime. Once again the Government's suspicions fell on
Harrison, and on Christmas Day he was re-arrested. During his
subsequent interrogation Harrison told Cromwell bluntly that he
strongly disapproved of the Government; but he assured him
that in no circumstances did he intend to conspire for its overthrow. Cromwell accepted this assurance, and Harrison was
released. However suspicion now fell on another prominent
soldier, Major-General Robert Overton. The latter was a scholar
as well as a soldier, and numbered John Milton amongst his
friends. A Yorkshireman, he had had a brilliant career in the
Parliamentary forces, and in 1653 had been appointed Governor
of Hull. By this time, however, he had become a fervent Fifth
Monarchy Man, and like Harrison, he was bitterly disappointed
when Barebone's Parliament came to an end, and Cromwell
assumed the title of Lord Protector. His dissatisfaction was
known to Cromwell; indeed, Overton had made no secret of it;
and so he was brought from Hull to London, and on 16 January
1655 imprisoned in the Tower.

Meanwhile, to add to Cromwell's troubles, in nearby Lambeth
Palace the recalcitrant John Rogers was stirring up trouble both
within and without his prison walls. Rogers wrote a detailed
account of the first months of his stay in Lambeth Palace in his

book *Jegar-Sahadutha: An Oyled Pillar*, published three years afterwards in July 1657. In this book he alleged that he was deprived of air and exercise by Serjeant Dendy, the chief gaoler, and that Dendy allowed others prisoners to torment him. Such a one was Abdy, 'a high ranter and blasphemer and atheist' who, Rogers alleged,

when he heard me at prayer in my family, he would come to the door shreeking, yelling and screaming with a most hideous noise, thump at the door, open it, and come in among us, singing, roaring, smoaking tobacco, cursing, swearing, blaspheming, blowing horns and the like, on purpose to disturb us. When we sung hymns, he would sing filthy blasphemous ribaldry in bawdy languages, and at every end of his sentence some desperate oath.[5]

Rogers declared that Abdy and his cronies were worse than the 'worst cavaliers or wickedest of men', and that he had made Lambeth Palace 'a very pourtraicture of Hell and Horrour'. Moreover, a very vile slander had been circulated to the effect that Rogers had played cards at Lambeth during Christmas, 1654.

The Cavalier prisoners [Rogers said] and the rest of the ranting crew in that prison did play, drink and game day and night, all the time; but for my part, I neither saw nor touch'd a pair of cards all the time. . . . I have had a kind of antipathy to cards ever since my suffering with the Puritans . . . and cannot endure to see a pair of cards: and if I see but any, anywhere, that I can lay hands of, I burn them![6]

A report was later sent to Whitehall, probably by Serjeant Dendy, concerning Rogers' complaints about his treatment in Lambeth Palace; and this reply put a different complexion on affairs. Rogers, it was said, preached continuously against the Government to 'a handfull of scum, the very raf of Billingsgate, Redriffe, Ratcliffe and Wappen', and, indeed, not in any 'misticall expressions, but in plaine words'. He told his listeners that the saints 'must shortly enjoy and possesse the glory of the earth', that 'the Antichrist, the Babilon, the great dragon or the

---

[5] *Jegar-Sahadutha*, p. 19 (Introduction).
[6] Ibid., p. 33.

man of sin, Oliver Cromwell in Whitehall, must be pul'd down',
and much else of 'such like fantasticque stuff'.[7]

The continued imprisonment of Rogers caused much distress
to the faithful members of his congregation, and on 29 January
1655 twelve of them sought an interview with Cromwell,[8] and
implored him, in the name of Jesus, to release 'the Lord's
prisoners', Rogers and Feake. Cromwell replied that the two
ministers were not imprisoned because of their beliefs, but because they were evildoers and busybodies, always trying to stir
up trouble. However, he declared, he would put the matter 'to
an issue', and have Rogers brought before him for a full and
frank discussion.

Accordingly on 6 February 1655 one of the most curious con-
frontations in English history took place in Whitehall. Early that
day many members of Rogers' congregation went to Lambeth
Palace to pray with and for him; and at three in the afternoon
about twenty, including his wife, accompanied him when he was
taken across the river to Whitehall. Only three or four of the
party, however, were admitted with Rogers into Cromwell's
presence; and the Lord Protector, who had assembled a number
of his own supporters to lend him aid in argument, if necessary,
went roundly into the charge by telling Rogers to his face that he
was kept in custody because he was a railer, a busybody, and a
stirrer-up of sedition. Certainly he was not detained 'for the
testimony of Jesus Christ'. Indeed, said Cromwell, no man in
England suffered for that.

At this Rogers made a pious gesture of dissent, and Cromwell
turned on him sharply. 'Nay, do not lift up your hands and your
eyes!' he exclaimed; and then repeated that nobody in England
suffered for the testimony of Jesus Christ. However, the Lord
Protector added, he was not prepared to allow such liberty to be
abused—not by anyone.

Rogers replied with equal vehemence that no law of God made
him an offender, but only Cromwell's—which was 'worse than
the Roman law and tyranny, that makes a man a traitor for

---

[7] Thurloe, *State Papers*, Vol. III, p. 136.

[8] Twelve were chosen because that was 'the Lamb's number
against the Beast, and the root and square number of the hundred
fourty-four thousand in Rev. 14'.

words'. Cromwell interrupted him at that, and demanded: 'Who calls you a traitor?' He then went on: '*I* call you not. See, I believe you speak many things according to the Gospel; but you suffer for evil doing!'

The Protector then declared that he would prove that Rogers was a railer, a liar, and a raiser of sedition; and he thereupon ordered that certain documents on a nearby table should be read aloud. Cromwell himself took one of the papers, the report on Rogers from Lambeth Palace, and read from it the passages which alleged that Rogers had publicly preached that Cromwell was the great dragon who sat in Whitehall, and must be pulled down.

Rogers denied having used such language, and said he would not answer 'such stuff' fabricated by people who had been basely bribed to inform against him. He demanded from Cromwell a fair hearing in a court of law; and he affirmed that if this took place he did not fear the outcome of it. He could not, he added, but mourn for Cromwell, surrounded as the Protector was by informers and other hirelings who deceived him for their own base ends. 'I think', he said, 'my condition, through Grace, though a poor prisoner, a great deal better than yours! I would not change with you!'

This moved Cromwell to anger. 'Well! Well!' he exclaimed. 'You are known well enough, and what spirit you are of. We know you; and to call your sufferings for Christ, when they are for evil-doing is not well; yea, it is blasphemy; yea, I say blasphemy again, for all your lifting up of your eyes!'

Rogers now declared solemnly to the Lord Protector, in the name of Jehovah, that his condition was very desperate. If he consulted the holy oracles he would find that the next vial of wrath which was due to be poured out would be scorching hot, and likely to fall upon the heads of Cromwell and the other 'apostate professors' who had forsaken and betrayed the cause of Christ. Cromwell's reply to this warning was short and sharp: 'Look you to *your* conscience', he observed, 'and I will look to mine!'

Continuing the theme of apostasy, Rogers alleged that the Army had most perfidiously betrayed the cause of Christ, and was therefore odious to the saints. Asked to give an example, he declared that the Army leaders had violated their declaration of

1647 against absolute power being vested in any one person. Cromwell interrupted angrily to ask: 'Who—hear me!—who, who, I say, hath broken that? Where is an arbitrary or absolute power?—Nay, hear me—where *is* such a Power?'

Rogers was quite undismayed by the Lord Protector's vehemence. 'Is not the long-sword such?' he asked in reply; and went on: 'Is not your power with the armies absolute, to break up Parliaments and do what you will?'

Rogers asserted that if God gave his call he, Rogers, for one, was ready to side with just principles, whether it should be by preaching, praying, or fighting. The struggle in England, he continued, was no longer, as it had been, between a king and his people; it was now between Cromwell and Christ. Let Cromwell judge, Rogers continued, which of these two was the higher Power, the one to which Rogers and his brethren should give their obedience.

'Ha!' said Cromwell, 'I heard indeed it is some of your principles to be at it. You long to be at it! You want but an opportunity!'

Rogers was unquelled, and aggressive. 'The Remnant of the Woman's Seed must be at it when they hear the call!' he replied, and then added, 'I beseech you, my Lord, consider how near it is to the end of the Beast's dominion, the forty-two months, and what time of day it is with us now!' This turn of the conversation, introducing Fifth Monarchy chronology, was not to Cromwell's liking, and he said sarcastically: 'Talk not of that, for I must tell you plainly that they are things I understand not!' These words played into Rogers' hand, however, and he at once complacently replied: 'It seems, my Lord, so, else surely you durst not lay violent hands upon us for the testimony and truth of the day, as you do!'

By now the dialogue had reached a dead end, and Cromwell said that he could spare no more time, since he had pressing public business to attend to. Before he dismissed Rogers and his supporters, however, he gave them a little homily. 'I tell you, there wants brotherly love!' he declared; and said that the different denominations and groups, the Anabaptists, the Fifth Monarchy Men, the Presbyterians, and others would be cutting one another's throats if he, the Protector, were not present to keep the peace.

Cromwell was now asked by one of the brethren to set Rogers free; but he refused to commit himself, saying that he would take his own time deciding what to do. The Lord Protector now departed; but as he walked to the door Rogers had the last word. Crying out after Cromwell, he warned him that he, the Lord Protector, would also be judged; that the day of the Lord was near; that he would find that Rogers and Feake would be proved true prophets; and that their words would come to pass ere long. . . .[9]

While the memorable meeting between Rogers and Cromwell was taking place, a large crowd of the former's supporters had assembled in the yard near the guardhouse. Among these were Major-General Harrison, Quartermaster-General Hugh Courtney, Colonel Nathaniel Rich, and Mr. John Carew. Courtney, like Harrison, had gained rapid promotion in the Parliamentary forces, and had become converted to Fifth Monarchy doctrines. John Carew, of an ancient Cornish family, was an ardent Parliamentarian and had been one of the judges who had condemned King Charles I to death. He strongly disapproved of the Protectorate, and his opposition to temporal power led him into the ranks of the Fifth Monarchy Men.

As Rogers passed through the yard on his way back to Lambeth Palace these sympathizers greeted him joyfully, and then, after he had gone, themselves sought an interview with Cromwell. This they were granted, and they at once pleaded that Rogers should be released. Their request was refused, and they were dismissed; but a few days later Cromwell asked them to come to Whitehall to hear from him at length his reasons for keeping Feake and Rogers in custody.

Harrison and his companions refused this invitation, and they

---

[9] A 'faithfull narrative' of Rogers' interview with the Lord Protector was later (21 March) published by his supporters 'to prevent mistakes and misreports thereupon'. It was addressed:
To the Faithful Remnant of the
Lamb, who are in this Day of great Rebuke and Blasphemy
ingaged against the BEAST and his GOVERNMENT,
especially to the New Non-Conforming Churches, and
Saints in City and Country, commonly called by the Name of
Fifth Monarchy Men.
It is reproduced in Rogers, *Some Account of the Life and Opinions of a Fifth Monarchy Man* (London 1867), Ch. VI.

likewise refused to comply with a warrant which was issued afterwards, requiring them to report to the Council of State. Because of their contumacy they were arrested on 16 February, and brought before the Council and Cromwell. They were first asked why they had refused to obey the warrant, and they replied that to have complied with it would have involved recognizing the Government. This they declined to do, for it was a Government set up against the will of God, and in opposition to the Kingdom of Christ. For good measure, Carew added that after Barebone's Parliament had been dissolved, Cromwell had taken the crown from Christ's head, and had placed it on his own.

The four recalcitrants then stated quite categorically that since in their opinion the Government could not be recognized, it was lawful to take up arms against it. Pressed to give a reason for their objection to the Government, they at once replied that it was 'because it had a Parliament in it, whereby power is derived from the people; whereas all power belongs to Christ!'

Even after these uncompromising declarations of hostility, Harrison, Courtney, Carew, and Rich were given one last chance. They were asked if they were prepared to give an undertaking that they would retire to their homes, and not stir up trouble. They all refused to give such an undertaking, and so were told that they would be imprisoned. Before they were taken away Cromwell spoke to each in turn, and told him why he was to suffer imprisonment: Harrison—because he had countenanced persons who had attacked the Government, and had persuaded others of the lawfulness of rebellion; Carew—the same as Harrison, but in addition Carew had tried to seduce some army officers from their allegiance; Rich—he had tried to hinder the raising of taxes; Courtney—he had done his best to foment rebellion in Norfolk and the West Country.

The four men stood silent while Cromwell made his accusations, and so, mute and defiant, they were taken away. A few days later Harrison was consigned to Portland Castle, Courtney to Carisbrooke, and Carew to Pendennis Castle in Cornwall. Rich, for the time being, was allowed his liberty as his wife lay dying.

While Harrison and his friends were defying the Protector in person, John Spittlehouse once again defended the cause of the saints in print. On 18 Feburary 1655 he published:

An
Answer
To one part of
The Lord Protector's Speech:
or
A Vindication
of the
Fifth Monarchy-men,
In reference to an Accusation of evil
charged upon them in his Speech to the
Parliament in the Painted Chamber,
the 4 of September 1654.

Cromwell, said Spittlehouse, had declared that the saints' conception of the imminence of the Fifth Monarchy was 'a mistaken notion'. 'I shall speak thereunto!' Spittlehouse announced with spirit; and he proceeded to do so, refuting Cromwell's assertions at considerable length.

The strictures passed by Spittlehouse and others against the Protector and his regime reflected faithfully the obstinacy with which the Fifth Monarchy Men adhered to their views, and their utter refusal to compromise. Once again, in fact, a familiar pattern had unfolded itself. By means of reasoned argument and discussion Cromwell had tried to dissipate the opposition of the Fifth Monarchy Men. He had failed; and so had had no alternative but to put the leaders under constraint. This course had, however, been tried before, to no avail; and once again, the only effect on the saints was to incite them to further acts of defiance.

5

TRIALS AND TRIBULATIONS

THE first Parliament of the Protectorate, which had assembled on 3 September 1654, and listened dutifully the next day to Cromwell's exhortations, proved as great a disappointment to the Protector, though for different reasons, as Barebone's Parliament had been. The Instrument of Government, under which the new Parliament had come into being, had set up a system of checks and balances between the executive and the legislature; but the new Parliament was not content to accept the constitution thus framed, and wanted to limit the powers of the Protector. Despite Cromwell's insistence that 'fundamentals' must not be called into question, the members persisted in debating a revision, and so on 22 January 1655 Cromwell dissolved the Parliament.

It was in these troubled circumstances that Rogers' defiant interview with Cromwell had taken place on 6 February; and the subsequent behaviour and attitude of Harrison, Rich, Carew, and Courtney reflected a widespread opposition to the Protector, in which not only Fifth Monarchy Men, but Levellers, Royalists, and others were involved. Plots against Cromwell's regime were discovered, and in March 1655 an attempt was made by the Royalist Colonel John Penruddock, at the head of a small force numbering about 180, to start an armed rebellion in Wiltshire. They failed to win popular support, however, and so marched westwards, but were defeated in Devonshire. Penruddock and other leaders were put to death, and about seventy other rebels were sentenced to transportation to the West Indies.

Though this Royalist rising had failed to get support, and had been easily suppressed, Cromwell took it as a warning signal, and in an endeavour to suppress opposition and prevent any future insurrections the Protector resorted to what was, in effect, military rule. He divided England and Wales into military districts, over each of which a Major-General was installed, with responsibility only to Cromwell and his Council. Though the existing administration was left untouched, the superimposition of the Major-Generals, who had command over the local militia, enabled Cromwell to maintain a firmer control over the country and keep malcontents under supervision. The first Major-General, in charge of the six south-western counties of England, was appointed in March 1655; and in October the whole country was subjected to the new system.

These developments fulfilled the worst expectations of 'the Lord's prisoners', John Rogers and Christopher Feake. Rogers, remitted to Lambeth after his confrontation with Cromwell, continued to prove such a nuisance to his gaolers, and such an embarrassment to the Government, that on 31 March 1655 the Council of State had him removed to Windsor Castle. No worse choice, however, from the Government's point of view, could conceivably have been made. Christopher Feake, known as a 'bold and crafty orator', had been held in Windsor Castle since January 1654; and to bring together two such men as Feake and Rogers was to ask for trouble. That trouble was made inevitable since, during the first month, Rogers was allowed freely to visit Feake in the latter's room. The visits were supposed to be for prayer; but there can be no doubt that each man supported and further incited the other's ingrained contempt for authority.

The results of this were soon evident. In April one of Feake's eight children (he had been allowed to take his family with him to Windsor) was reported to the Governor of the castle for having called Oliver Cromwell a fool. When the Governor took Feake to task for this the latter did not deny it; and added disrespectfully that he himself would go a step further and affirm that Cromwell was a tyrant. Rogers, standing by, nodded approvingly—at which the Governor threatened to have him put in a dungeon.

The next day, a Sunday, to punish Rogers and Feake, the Governor refused to allow their friends within the castle to visit them. On hearing this Feake and Rogers went to the castle chapel, just before morning service was due to begin, and Feake ascended the pulpit, from which he began to pray, with Rogers standing by. The Governor, informed of this insubordinate conduct, now appeared with a squad of soldiers. 'Pull him down! Pull him down!' he cried out furiously, staring up at Feake, and a soldier moved to obey the order. Rogers now sprang to the door at the foot of the pulpit steps, and held it closed. The soldiers forced him roughly aside, however, and then mounted the pulpit steps and dragged the protesting Feake down by force. Both men were then taken away to their quarters, where they were locked in with sentinels posted outside to make doubly sure that they did not break loose.

Even this summary treatment did not dampen their defiance, however; and Feake began to preach from his window in a loud voice so that Rogers, a little distance away, was able to hear him clearly. Feake continued to preach thus until the service in the castle chapel had ended, and the Governor and the congregation passed the prisoners' rooms on their way back. Some of the congregation lingered to hear the words coming from the window; whereupon the Governor had some drummers fetched, and commanded them to beat their drums continuously to drown Feake's voice. The orator was not to be intimidated, however.

As soon as the drum had done [Feake later recounted] then I began to sound out my trumpet, and trumpeted out the Gospel aloud; he [the Governor] beat up his drum a second and third time, and still I went on, then he strictly required me to have done. I told him, I would not. He said he had order to silence me from the Lord Protector. I told him, I had order from My Lord to go on; and my Lord's Highness is above his lord's highness.[1]

The drums continued to roll, and to give Feake some respite Rogers took over during the pauses, continuing the sermon at the point where Feake's voice had been drowned by the beating of the drums. By now it was nearly midday and the Governor was tired of this endurance test. Moreover, he was hungry, and his lunch awaited him. He accordingly departed, leaving Feake still preaching loudly and lustily from his window. 'Strange Government', the unrepentant pastor later remarked, 'that men's mouths must be stopped from preaching!'[1]

In the afternoon Rogers began to preach in a loud voice from his window, and this renewal of the verbal onslaught proved too much for the Governor. A sergeant and some soldiers were sent to deal with Rogers, in order to silence him. They entered his

---

[1] Thurloe, *State Papers*, Vol. V, pp. 756–7.

room, seized him, tore off his cloak, and beat him hard. The only response however was a cry: 'Strike on, for thus did the soldiers deal with Christ, my master!'

On a later occasion, on 8 May 1655, Rogers was praying loudly in his room when Feake, guarded by soldiers and on his way 'to ease nature' as Rogers put it, halted to listen to the prayers. The guard commander ordered the soldiers to pull Feake away, but the sergeant in the detachment refused, declaring that his conscience would not allow him to do it. Thereupon the guard commander struck the sergeant with his sword, still in its scabbard, with such force that (according to Rogers' account of the incident)[2] he 'brake his brain-pan'. After this the other soldiers, through fear, obeyed the guard commander and dragged Feake away.

As usual, Feake and Rogers were loud in their protestations about the harsh and brutal treatment to which they alleged they were subjected in Windsor Castle; and as a result on 16 May 1655 commissioners were sent from Whitehall to investigate the complaints. Rogers and Feake, before giving evidence, insisted—characteristically—on seeing a copy of the commission. When this was refused on the grounds that they declined to recognize the legitimacy of the Government, they would not answer any of the commissioners' questions; and so in the end everyone was heard except the two complainants themselves. 'They' [the commissioners] went home with a flea in their ear, it seems,' Rogers remarked, 'but well fraught with informations against us to their master!'[3]

Despite the ill-reports which must have been carried to Whitehall, Rogers and Feake were allowed to remain in Windsor Castle for a few more months. Then on 1 October 1655 they were transferred to Sandown Castle in the Isle of Wight. Rogers, like Feake, had been allowed to keep his wife and family with him in Windsor, and Mrs. Rogers was in the last stages of pregnancy when the order to move came. Nevertheless, Rogers was forced to leave her. 'Notwithstanding I wanted necessaries', he recounted later, 'and had not riding-coat, boots, or things fit for such a journey. Yet with musketeers and officers they fetched me out of

---

[2] *Jegar-Sahadutha*, p. 9.
[3] Ibid., p. 9.

my chamber by violence, and rent me from my weak wife in childbed, and weeping babes and children about me.'[4]

Despite these emotional upsets, however, Rogers had enough presence of mind to take some precautions, 'conveying', so he said, 'a few of my papers into the bottome of my stockins at the soals of my feet, to preserve them from their hands and searches'.[5]

Rogers and Feake were forcibly mounted on their horses, and the cavalcade, if Rogers is to be believed, departed from Windsor amidst the lamentations of the inhabitants. 'The poore people on both sides of the streets standing weeping, lifting up their eyes, blessing, pittying and praying for us as we passed through, to see us so carried and hurried into banishment for the name of Christ!'[6]

The party rested the first night at Farnham, the next at Alton, and the third at Portsmouth. From here they crossed to Sandown Castle on the Isle of Wight, and here Rogers and Feake had for a time to sleep on the floor in their clothes till beds were procured from Newport for them. The conditions were so bad at Sandown that even the soldiers, so Feake said, 'melted over' with pity. There was, he continued, when he spoke later about his experiences:

only one pitifull bed so damp that it had been enough to have spoyled us had we made use of it; and though we might have aired it, yet it was too bad to lie on, being stuffed both bed and bolster with hops; yet one of our keepers told us a hop-bed was as good as down, besides that a pillow of hops was good for the head; but we chose rather to lye upon the boards, and to make use of stools, without pulling off our cloaths. And in all the time I was supported with this consideration, that it was the case once of good Nehemiah, a great man and a governor. The words out of the 4th of Nehemiah, the last verses, are these:

'So neither I nor my brethren, nor my servants, nor the men of the guard which followed me, none of us put off our cloaths, save that every one put them off for washing.'

This text was a great comfort to us. The truth is, our condition was such there, . . . that many of the soldiers wept![7]

---

[4] Ibid., p. 19.   [5] Ibid., p. 19.
[6] Ibid., p. 19.
[7] Thurloe, *State Papers*, Vol. V, p. 757.

After their privations at Sandown, Feake and Rogers were moved to a private dwelling, Afton House, near Freshwater, and finally, in December, to Carisbrooke Castle. Major-General Harrison and Quartermaster-General Courtney had been confined in this castle since the early part of 1655 (Harrison having been moved there from Portland Castle at the beginning of April), and they lost no time in welcoming the new arrivals. 'The next morning', Rogers wrote later, 'came my dear con-captives (for this most noble and excellent cause of the King of Saints) to see me, Maj. Gen. Harrison and Mr. Courtney, who were a long time kept up in this close gaol. . . .'[8]

Fortified by the company of these illustrious prisoners, and undismayed by the memory of what had happened at Windsor, Rogers began to preach within the castle precincts, and since for some time no objection was raised to this, people soon began to come from places nearby to listen to his sermons. Because of the subversion which he propagated, however, his preaching was soon stopped, and he was confined to his room, with sentries on guard outside.

Rogers now resorted to his former stratagem of preaching through the window; and according to his own account the soldiers themselves listened and were much affected. Because of this, Bull, the head gaoler, was enraged, and as a punishment deprived Rogers of his bed. Later, Rogers, his wife, maid-servant, and children (who by now had been allowed to rejoin him in Carisbrooke) were, he alleged, shamefully ill-treated by soldiers at the instigation of the infamous Bull.

While the leaders of the Fifth Monarchy Men languished in confinement, the cause of the saints continued to be sedulously disseminated by those who remained at liberty. In November Major-General Goffe, who had responsibility for Berkshire, Sussex, and Hampshire under Cromwell's new system, reported that a minister named Postlethwaite in Lewes, who was 'of Mr. Feake's principles', and preached to the largest congregation in the town, publicly 'bewailed the imprisonment of the saint'. In a letter to Secretary Thurloe on 7 November Goffe went even further, and said that 'the generallity of the professors of religion' in Lewes were much discontented over the imprisonment of

---

[8] *Jegar-Sahadutha*, p. 19.

Feake and Harrison; and he added that nothing would satisfy them but the release of the captives.[9]

In the autumn of 1655 another notorious Fifth Monarchy agitator, Vavasor Powell, was still travelling around his native Wales, preaching against the Government; and in November he drew up a petition to Cromwell which was signed by more than three hundred of his followers. The petition, 'against wickedness in high places', contained insinuations against the Protector's regime, and Powell was accordingly run to earth at last, and brought before Major-General Berry in Worcester. Berry, however, was impressed by Powell's sincerity and well-meant, if misguided, intentions; and after talking to him in a sympathetic manner, allowed him to return to Wales, on condition that he promised to be of good behaviour in the future.

Though Powell for the time being at least had been subdued, more was to be heard of the petition he had organized. It was printed, and on 3 December was publicized in the pulpit of Allhallows, Upper Thames Street, by the old firebrand John Simpson, aided and abetted by one Cornet Day. Simpson and Day used the occasion to castigate Cromwell and his Government in traditional style. In a letter, dated from Whitehall on 17 December, addressed to Cromwell's son Henry, then in Ireland, Thurloe related:

Cornet Day and Mr. John Sympson preached or rather rayled there [Allhallows], and did it in such scurrilous language that all this towne ringes of it. The best termes they gave us at Whitehall were, the theeves and robbers at Whitehall, and the great theife Oliver Cromwell, the tyrant and usurper; which expressions they used above 20 tymes, *cum multis aliis*, stirring up the people to action against the Government.[10]

Thurloe added that Cornet Day had been secured, but that Simpson had managed to avoid arrest and had gone into hiding. In another letter to Henry Cromwell, from Whitehall on 25 December 1655, Thurloe wrote:

I doe assure you that his highness [Cromwell] is put to exercise every day with the peevishness and wrath of some persons heere. But the Lord enables hym with comfort to beare the hard speeches

---

[9] Thurloe, *State Papers*, Vol. IV, pp. 151, 161.   [10] Ibid., p. 321.

and reproaches which he is loaded with from day to day; and helps
hym to returne good for evill, and good will for their hatred.[11]

This was indeed true, and Thurloe did not exaggerate Cromwell's magnanimity. Few Englishmen, not even the Royalists,
can have directed against him 'peevishness and wrath' more con-
sistently than the Fifth Monarchy Men; yet Cromwell continued
to treat them like naughty, misguided children whom he dis-
ciplined against his will, and whom he did not wish to keep in
confinement a day longer than was necessary.

Thus on 19 February 1656 the Protector and his Council
decided to release Harrison, Carew, Courtney, and Rich from
their imprisonment, and this decision was postponed only because of reports brought to Whitehall at this time that the Fifth
Monarchy Men in London were plotting to take up arms against
the Government. Already in November 1655 Thurloe had
written to Henry Cromwell stating: 'It is certeyne that the 5th
monarchy men (some of them I mean) have designes of puttinge
us into blood.'[12]

Plotting was going on in February 1656 to raise rebellion in
London and the provinces, although not every Fifth Monarchy
Man, as Thurloe had noted, was in favour of taking drastic
action. A notable and highly unexpected dissentient was John
Simpson, who told a meeting in London on 18 February that he
was utterly against resort to arms. Despite this strange and un-
accountable volte-face by one who had been numbered among
the more intransigent brethren, the plotting went on; and
Government informants reported that young men and appren-
tices in large numbers were daily resorting to Swan Alley, Coleman Street, in the City, to listen to inflammatory sermons and
speeches by the Fifth Monarchy Men.

For example, on Sunday 23 March one John Jones declared
to a large assembly in the Swan Alley meeting-place that the
Government was oppressing the saints of God by keeping many
worthy brethren such as Major-Generals Harrison and Overton
in prison. Jones then called on his listeners to be firm in their
faith, and to use all their endeavours to pluck down the existing
power, which was an idol set up amongst them, and part of the
evil Fourth Monarchy.

---

[11] Ibid., p. 343.   [12] Ibid., p. 191.

The fears of the Government were reinforced when other informants alleged that Colonel John Okey had been present at the meetings. In November 1654 Okey had been cashiered because of his opposition to Cromwell, and had afterwards consorted more and more closely with the Fifth Monarchy Men. Reports that a soldier of his courage, experience, and religious fanaticism was taking part in the Swan Alley meetings must not unnaturally have caused the Government serious concern.

Nevertheless, if any plans for an insurrection were actually concerted by the Fifth Monarchy Men, they must have been dropped, perhaps because of the opposition of John Simpson and others. At all events, the Government felt sufficiently reassured by 22 March, the day before John Jones demanded the release of Harrison, to order that the latter should be freed from his imprisonment. About the same time the Council of State also commanded that Colonel Nathaniel Rich, too, should be released.

Before Harrison, who was freed from Carisbrooke against his will, was sent to his father-in-law's home in Highgate, he took a sorrowful farewell of his fellow-prisoners. John Rogers, one of these, remarked of the occasion: 'We parted (as the sun through a watry cloud) with no little heaviness for a season'—and the saints remaining in Carisbrooke spent the whole of the remainder of the day in prayer on behalf of their departed brother.

The appearance of Harrison in Highgate gave new hope to the Fifty Monarchy Men. Soon there were regular visits to the released Prisoner of the Lord, and at the meeting-place in Swan Alley, Coleman Street, the propagation of the sect's doctrines was carried on with renewed vigour. On 25 May, for example, one John Gardiner declared that the Fifth Monarchy Men were God's elect, chosen by the Almighty from the rest of the nation, the Laodicean majority who had apostasized and accepted a hypocritical government. However, Gardiner added, the time of deliverance was near; and he counselled his listeners to be as the lion, terrible to the rest of the beasts. He quoted Deuteronomy xxxii. 41–43 to make his meaning perfectly clear:

If I whet my glittering sword, and mine hand take hold on judgement; I will render vengeance to mine enemies, and will reward them that hate me.
I will make mine arrows drunk with blood, and my sword shall

devour flesh; and that with the blood of the slain and of the captives, from the beginning of revenges upon the enemy.

Rejoice, O ye nations, with his people; for he will avenge the blood of his servants, and will render vengeance to his adversaries, and will be merciful unto his land, and to his people.

The Lord, Gardiner triumphantly concluded, was even now preparing to triumph over his enemies, and to own that handful of faithful people, the saints, and act wonderfully by them.

Another speaker at the meeting on 25 May railed against Cromwell and the Army. Formerly, he declared, there had been many godly men in the Army; but they had gorged themselves with lands owned in the past by the King and the bishops, and were now tyrants who laid heavy taxes on the people. At this the congregation were much moved, and wept, sighed, and groaned; but the speaker cheered them up by adding that he hoped he would live long enough to see the day when the Lion of Judah conquered the present apostate rulers and drove them before him like a flock of sheep.

By July the threats to overturn the Government by force had led to the beginnings of organized revolt. At a meeting of the Fifth Monarchy Men in the City on 8 July it was agreed that the time had come at last to pull down Babylon by force, and that the saints must do it. Five groups, each of about twenty-five members meeting separately, were organized, and it was decided that one member of each group should be chosen as leader, to whom full details were regularly to be supplied by the other members of the group of their arms, money resources, and availability for immediate action. The leader of each group was to transmit this information only to the leaders of the other groups, without mentioning any names. Thus everybody connected with the enterprise would be kept constantly informed of the progress of the preparations, and the state of readiness, but very few people would be compromised should details of the plot leak out.

To enlarge the scope of the projected revolt contact was made with the Commonwealth Men, a group who favoured strict republicanism based on democratically-elected parliaments, and who were as bitterly hostile to Cromwell as the Fifth Monarchy Men were. In a conference with representatives of the Commonwealth Men which took place early in July, Thomas Venner seems to have been chief spokesman for the Fifth Monarchy Men.

Venner, a London wine-cooper, had emigrated to New England in 1638, but had returned in 1651 and become a Fifth Monarchy enthusiast, although for a number of years he remained in obscurity. About 1655 he was employed in the Tower of London —in what capacity is not known—but was dismissed because of the reports which came to the authorities of his subversive speeches at the meeting-place in Swan Alley and elsewhere.

The conference with the Commonwealth Men considered a tract entitled *A Healing Question Propounded and Resolved* recently produced by Sir Henry Vane. Vane was the eldest son of Sir Henry Vane of Hadlow in Kent, who had been Secretary of State to Charles I. Despite this background the younger Vane espoused the cause of Parliament, and became a leading member of the Commons, notable for his opposition to episcopacy. He took no part in the trial of Charles I, but became a member of the Council of State of the Commonwealth. He continued to sit as a member of the Rump, but earned Cromwell's especial disapproval as one of the members of that body who supported the proposal that sitting members should automatically become members of the next Parliament. Vane was among those expelled on 20 April 1653, and he then retired to his estate in Lincolnshire, where he devoted himself to private studies and religious meditations. Though it is virtually impossible to define his religious beliefs, as set forth diffusely in his book *The Retired Man's Meditations* (1655), there can be no doubt that he was considerably influenced by Fifth Monarchy doctrines, and held millenarian views, which were set forth in Chapter 26 of his book.

In secular affairs, however, Vane was an advocate of the sovereignty of elected parliaments; and so when Fifth Monarchists and Commonwealth Men at their meeting in July 1656 took Vane's *Healing Question* as a possible basis for collaboration, the prospects of agreement might well have seemed favourable. The full title of Vane's tract, published on 12 May 1656, was: 'A Healing Question propounded and resolved upon occasion of the late publique and seasonable Call to Humiliation, in order to love and union among the honest party, and with a desire to apply balsome to the wound, before it become incurable.'

Vane said that the great problem was to consider first what possibility remained of uniting all 'honest men within the three nations' who professed to believe in 'the good old cause'; and secondly, how to effect this union. His solution was the summoning of a constituent assembly elected by the 'whole body of adherents' of 'the good old cause'; and in a postscript he added that he had put forward his proposals so that the various groups who had the 'good old cause' at heart might 'with better satisfaction meet together, and agree upon a safe and righteous bottome, then to remain at the distance they doe, to the apparent advantage of the Common Enemie, the approaching ruine of themselves, and needless hazard (if not losse) of the cause they have been so deeply engaged in'.

The advice in Vane's *Healing Question* went unheeded, and the discussions between the Fifth Monarchy and the Commonwealth Men foundered. The latter, not unreasonably, wanted all details of the proposed new Government—its nature, the method of choosing it, and so on—to be settled beforehand. Moreover, hankering after legality, they suggested that some forty carefully selected members of the old Long Parliament should be brought together to give a semblance of constitutional propriety to the revolt which was envisaged.

Venner and the other Fifth Monarchists would have none of this. They were thirsting for action, and felt no desire to shelter under any other kind of authority than their divine mandate to inaugurate the rule of the saints. As for the composition and powers of the future government—those and other details, they felt, could safely be left to the providence of God.

The discussions between the Fifth Monarchy and the Commonwealth Men were, in fact, inevitably doomed to fail, since the meeting was one of unlike minds. On the one hand there were pragmatic realists; but on the other, visionary fanatics. Nevertheless great efforts were made to bring the two groups together; and finally Major-General Harrison and Colonel Rich were invited to attend the discussions to try to reconcile the differences. Both Harrison and Rich, however, thought the project so hopeless that they prudently refused to be associated with the plotters in any way.

It was just as well; for informants brought news of the meetings to the Government, and on 29 July an order was issued for the arrest of the ringleaders. Venner escaped in time and went into hiding, but the chief representatives of the Commonwealth Men were apprehended, although they were soon released, after an examination before the Council of State.

The same clemency was not shown to Sir Henry Vane. The Council of State decided that the *Healing Question* was a 'seditious book . . . tending to the disturbance of the present Government and the peace of the Commonwealth'; and he was therefore ordered to appear before the Council on 29 July. Defiantly, he informed the Council's clerk that it was contrary to the rights of an Englishman to have to obey such a summons. In reply, on 21 August the Council of State decreed that if Vane did not deposit £5000 as a security for his good conduct in future, he should be taken into custody. Vane refused to comply, and so on 4 September the Council ordered that he should be arrested and sent to Carisbrooke Castle. Here he met a kindred spirit in the person of the still incarcerated and impenitent John Rogers, and the two soon became close companions.

In August Colonel Rich, too, had once again fallen under suspicion, and had been committed on the eighth of the month to Windsor Castle. In the autumn, however, the Government began to relax its security measures, and on 14 October the Council of State ordered that Rich should be released, but confined to his house at Eltham. At the same time Quartermaster-General Courtney was allowed to leave Carisbrooke.

Christopher Feake, largely because of his wife's ill-health, had been liberated from imprisonment in the Isle of Wight, and transferred to a private dwelling on the mainland, where he was ordered to stay until further notice. Feake had, in effect, been put on his honour to repay the Government's clemency with obedience, since no guard was appointed to watch over him. He interpreted Cromwell's leniency, however, in his own peculiar way. The Protector, he said, had been pleased to appoint him as his own gaoler; and this led Feake to remark: 'Such an unnatural order, I think, was never heard before!'

Accordingly, as was his wont, Feake sought inspiration from the Scriptures to find out what he should do next:

At length [he afterwards related] came into my mind the case of Peter and John in the 4th of the Acts, who being called before the High Priest Ananias and Caiaphas, were by them commanded not to preach in the name of Jesus. Now suppose, that either of their highnesess had sent Peter and John an order, enjoyning them to confine themselves to such a village as Saron, or Joppa, or the like, and forbear coming to preach at Jerusalem, suppose, I say, an order had come to them upon that account, signed by either of their highnesses Ananias H, or Caiaphas H, like this [order of Cromwell's] with Oliver P, do you think they would have obeyed it, and been confined to a village? We find the contrary, for they preached the more boldly in the city of Jerusalem. Then [Feake triumphantly and complacently concluded] having my warrant here from the Scriptures, I resolved for London, notwithstanding the order of Oliver P![13]

Despite this act of ingratitude and defiance, Feake was afterwards permitted to live in his own house in London; but this time a guard was put over him to prevent any more escapades. 'This', said Feake, who was always able to console himself with biblical parallels, 'did the less trouble me, when I remembered it was once the condition of Paul, in the same kind, to have a soldier attending upon him.'

Though Feake was now kept under close surveillance, he managed somehow to continue his written polemics against the Protector, and to get these into his friends' hands so that they could be printed. On 22 September 1656 a Fifth Monarchy pamphlet was published in London by one who signed himself 'a well-wisher to the Kingdom of our Lord Jesus', under the following title:

The Prophets
Malachy and Isaiah
Prophecying
to
The Saints and Professors of this Generation
of
The Great Things the Lord will doe
in this their Day and Time.

Feake and another Fifth Monarchy preacher called John Pendarves contributed prefaces to the pamphlet; and Feake, for his part, excelled himself in abusing Cromwell. On the Day of Judgement, he declared, Cromwell would stand before Jesus Christ without his clergy or lawyers to plead his cause, and, Feake continued:

---

[13] Thurloe, *State Papers*, Vol. V, p. 757.

We shall understand then what instructions they were which he or his secretaries gave his catchpoles when he imployed them, and what conference he had with them when they read our sermon notes in his hearing; and all those works of darknesse and secrecy shall be brought to light, and our Lord himself shall second our testimony that their Deeds were evill. . . . It is not to be expected that his Highnesses Court Chaplaines who are fed at his Table, should lift up their heel against their Good Lord and Master, in testifying openly that his counsells are evill, that his *Instrument* is an ugly Idol, and an Image of Jealousie, that his Government is evill, that his workes in imprisoning the Servants of Christ without just cause are evill, that his extortion and rapine in imposing and gathering in all his taxes by an arbitrary power, contrary to the Law of God and the Land, is evill. . . .

The 'inslaved preachers', Feake said, who received 'the ancient profits and perquisites of the parish' for truckling to Cromwell, were poor wretches who had not the courage to protest against the 'new invented Babylonish abominations'. But, Feake asserted, the saints, the prisoners of the Lord, were not frightened 'to bid Defyance to the scarlet coloured Beast, and to all his 7 heads of Blasphemy and to all his ten horns of persecution!'

As a final parting shot of defiance the tirade was signed: 'Christopher Feake: From mine own Hired House (where a souldier is appointed to keep me) this 14 day of the 5 month, 1656.' (Old style; by modern reckoning, 14 July.)

Despite these venomous rantings, Feake, by a decision of the Council of State on 11 December 1656, was freed from all constraint; and at the same time John Rogers and Sir Henry Vane were released from their imprisonment in the Isle of Wight. Vane departed to his home in Lincolnshire, and resumed his religious meditations. Rogers and Feake, however, once again repaid the Government for its leniency by forthwith resuming, from the pulpit, their denunciations of the Protector and his regime.

Imprisonment had had absolutely no effect on them, except to make them more angry and fanatical than ever, and they used their liberty to denounce Cromwell and his Government in ever more bitter and violent language, until they reached the stage of openly inciting their listeners to rebellion. Thus they played no little part in fanning into flame the embers of the plot which

Venner and the more militant Fifth Monarchy Men had tried to kindle in vain in May–July 1656. Incited by Rogers and Feake, the wild men of the sect were now impatient, as Rogers counselled them, to be ' up and doing' for the sake of the Lord.

6

DESPERATE ZEALOTS

By May 1656 Cromwell's Government was in financial difficulties. The burden of taxation, and the discontent provoked by the regime of the Major-Generals brought into being an increasing agitation for the summoning of a new Parliament; and though Cromwell, through bitter experience, was reluctant to give way to this, the state of the finances finally induced him in June to agree. The new Parliament met on 17 September 1656, after about one hundred members had been excluded because the Council of State objected to them as potential trouble-makers.

In accordance with custom, Cromwell gave an address to the newly-assembled Parliament in the Painted Chamber, in which he discoursed on the state of the nation. He spoke about the various groups which opposed his regime, and referred among others to the Levellers and the Commonwealth Men, whose doctrines were plain, if repugnant to him. As for the Fifth Monarchy Men, whose ideas were equally obnoxious, the Protector declared ironically that they were 'more seraphical'. To impress the members of Parliament with the weight of responsibility which rested upon them, Cromwell went on to give a warning that all the opposition groups were working to overthrow the Government, and to bring the country down to ruin and disaster.

The opposition of the Fifth Monarchy Men to the regime had been intensified by the Council of State's arbitrary exclusion of members from Parliament, and on 24 September 1656 a pamphlet appeared under the title:

The Banner of Truth Displayed:
Or, a
Testimony for Christ,
and against
Anti-Christ

Being the Substance of severall Consultations holden and kept by a Certain Number of CHRISTIANS, who are waiting for the visible appearance of CHRIST'S KINGDOME, in and over the world; and residing in and about the City of LONDON.

The writers, who for reasons of prudence did not give their names, began by declaring that 'Divine Providence... hath so ordered that our lot is faln out in the last dayes'; and they stated that in view of the imminence of Christ's return to take possession of his kingdom he must be proclaimed the only lawful ruler of the three nations. The 'Beast-like powers now in being' were traitors, and action would be taken against them in due course in accordance with the laws of King Jesus. Authority in the State, the writers affirmed, should reside only with the saints, because:

The Saints of the Most High... are a people distinct from the world... and are by themselves a Common-Wealth and Free-State; and therefore 'tis to be desired from good and found grounds, that they would exercise that Royal Authority which God has given unto them, and invested them with, as they are saints by calling.

The conclusion drawn from this divine commission was that it was lawful for the saints to use all honest and just means to defend themselves and to 'offend their enemies'. The authors of the pamphlet had no doubts about who the enemies were. 'The man of sin is still in the seat of authority', they said, and they went on to stigmatize his Government as oppressive and anti-christian. The oppression, they said, would vanish only when the Fourth Monarchy was totally destroyed, and the Fifth set up in its stead. The saints must therefore appear 'in a military posture for Christ', and 'do smiting work'. The time for this had not quite come; but the saints were to hold themselves constantly in readiness for the call; and meanwhile, they must watch and pray.

Similar denunciations of Cromwell and his Government were poured forth at the meetings of the Fifth Monarchy Men, since Feake and Rogers, their most prominent orators, were now, owing to the Government's leniency, back in the City and thus able to encourage the lesser brethren by their bitter diatribes. On Sunday, 4 January 1657 Feake had begun what he called 'the work of the Lord' at Newgate Market, when the City Marshal and a detachment of his men suddenly appeared, and hauled the protesting preacher away. He was later released,

however; and the next day, undeterred, attended a packed meeting at Allhallows Church in Upper Thames Street.

After lengthy prayers had been said Feake mounted the pulpit
for a marathon performance that was to last three hours. He
began by recounting how, three years before, he had been taken
into custody for preaching the Gospel in that very place; and
then had been incarcerated in various prisons. However, he
assured his listeners, despite his tribulations he was still 'as zealous
as ever against Babylon'. For, he declared, the Government was
as Babylonish as ever, and was in fact as bad as the old monarchy
had been, being sustained only by the Army.

After giving an unconscionably long-winded account of his
alleged sufferings in Windsor and the Isle of Wight, Feake
turned on those brethren who, so he said, had listened to
scandalous reports that he and his wife had been released from
Carisbrooke because of base compliance with the 'present
Powers'. 'They that love the Lord should love one another!'
Feake declaimed indignantly against the backbiters; and he
added that they should be 'tender how they raise or receive
reports one of another, especially concerning any that are
engaged in carrying on the work of the Lord!'

Having defended himself against the calumnies spread by his
enemies, Feake delivered a virulent attack upon the Government.
He declared that Antichrist still had his throne in Church and
State, and asserted that the Army gave as much support to
popery as ever King Charles and his bishops had done. The good
old cause had been forsaken by a corrupt company of priests,
lawyers, and soldiers, and there was 'Babylon civil and Babylon
ecclesiastick' in the nation.

Towards the end of his discourse he turned to the clerical
critics of the Fifth Monarchy theorists.

To me it seems strange [he observed] that this very day some
Independent ministers said, that they are fools who busy themselves in meddling with two such obscure books as the prophecy of
Daniel, and the Revelation. Lord have mercy upon us! Not meddle
with the Revelation, when we are commanded to search into it, and
understand it! But will you know the reason? There is so much of
Babylon laid open in it, so much of Babylon discovered there, in the
civil powers of the world, and in the worldly church, the parish
churches, and the national churches . . . and all the great jurisdic-

tions, and against all the parish-priests and tithe-mongers, that it is no wonder they do not care to have men looking into the Revelation!

Even now Feake had not done. Facing the crowded congregation, which included many women standing on chairs to get a better view of the preacher, he suddenly reverted to a topic which evidently rankled. He referred once again to the false reports about himself which had been circulated during his imprisonment; and he now pugnaciously challenged anyone in the assembly to stand up and repeat them, or to seek to justify them.

Nobody took up this challenge, and for a few moments there was silence. Then, however, a Mr. Jeffey arose, and stated boldly that he disagreed with what Feake had said about renting and dividing the churches. Mr. Jeffey was supported by Mr. Kiffin, and by the well-known preacher John Simpson, who for his part objected to Feake's fastening the terms 'antichristian' and 'Babylonish' on the civil Government. That was a doctrine which had dangerous implications.

At this point many people in the congregation took Feake's side, and some called out that Kiffin was a Government sycophant, whilst others denounced Simpson as an apostate, who had formerly preached in that very church the doctrines which he now criticized. The ensuing uproar became so great that further discussion was impossible; but Simpson and Kiffin stoutly maintained that they would be ready to defend their views on a more suitable occasion in the future. Feake thereupon brought the proceedings to an end with a prayer in which, determined to have the last word, he once again ranted and railed against those who opposed him.[1]

In the first week of January 1657 a plot was discovered to assassinate Cromwell by shooting at him with a blunderbuss whilst he was on his way to Hampton Court. Some obscure Fifth Monarchy Men and discontented Army officers were involved in this, and were arrested; but this fiasco did not deter the larger group of Fifth Monarchy Men who under Venner's direction had been preparing since the autumn of 1656 for armed insurrection to establish the rule of the saints.

In an account of this attempted rising which the Secretary of

---

[1] Thurloe, *State Papers*, Vol. V, pp. 755–9.

State, John Thurloe, later compiled, he rightly described it as 'a
designe of a very strange nature, and built upon very extraordinary pretences'.[2] Venner, the instigator and leader, was followed by only some eighty Fifth Monarchy Men, who, Thurloe
said, were 'mean fellows of noe note, but such as had blowne up
one another by a weekly meeting they had at a place called
Swan Alley in Coleman Street'.[3]

Their numbers may have been small, but their fanaticism was
great, and if Thurloe is to be believed, they fortified themselves
with brave words. 'They encouraged one another', Thurloe said,
'with this—that though they were but a worme, that yet they
should be made instrumental to thresh mountains!'[3]

A good deal of information about the preparations made for
the revolt has survived in a government transcript of a journal,
probably kept by Venner himself, in which the deliberations
and decisions of the conspirators were carefully noted down.[4]
From the journal it is clear that by January 1657 Venner and
his associates were busy settling the details of the insurrection.
Till then Christopher Feake had attended meetings; but probably because the plotters did not follow his advice he then
fell out with them, and took no further part in their deliberations.

After Feake's withdrawal they chose a committee of ten to
draw up a plan of action which could be put into action speedily;
and as a result the following decisions were made. First, the
rebels were to have a standard, and a seal, which should show a
lion couchant, surrounded by the words: 'Who shall rouse him
up?' Secondly it was decided that a declaration should be
drawn up, and that this should be printed so that copies of it
could be distributed as soon as the revolt had begun.

The declaration, prepared to justify and publicize the revolt,
and to attract adherents to the cause, was headed as follows:

A Standard
Set Up
Whereunto the true Seed and Saints of the Most High may be
gathered together into one, out of their several Forms.

---

[2] Thurloe, *State Papers*, Vol. VI, pp. 184–5.
[3] Ibid.
[4] British Museum Add. MS. 4459 fol. 111–22, reproduced in
the *English Historical Review* (1910), pp. 722–47.

For the Lambe against the Beast, and False Prophet in
this good and Honourable Cause.

Underneath the above title, which was signed 'W. Medley,
Scribe', were printed five relevant texts:

Gen. xlix, 9: Who shall rouse him up?

Deut. xxxiii, 27: The Eternall God is thy Refuge, and underneath
are the everlasting arms; and he shall thrust out
the Enemy from before thee, and shall say, Destroy
them.

Isaiah lx, 22: A little one shall become a thousand, and a small
one a strong Nation: I the Lord will hasten it in
his time.

Isaiah lxii, 10: Lift up a STANDARD for the People.

Rev. xix, 2: For True and Righteous are his Judgements, for
he hath judged the great Whore which did corrupt the Earth with her Fornication, and hath
avenged the Blood of his Servants at her hand.

The tract recounted the events which led up to the rule of the
godly Barebone's Parliament. This assembly had been unlawfully ended, and then Oliver Cromwell had committed the
'horrible sin' of exalting himself and his own interest. In 'bind-
ing his iron yoak upon the neck of the poor captive daughter of
Zion' he was guilty of high treason, for the only 'absolute single
person' to whom all power had been given by God was Jesus
Christ.

The declaration next explained how the country ought to be
governed. A Sanhedrim or Supreme Council of men 'of choicest
light and spirit' should be chosen to represent 'the whole Body of
the Saints', and should govern according to the precepts to be
found in the Scriptures. The Sanhedrim was to be re-elected each
year, by 'the Lord's Freemen—those who have a right with
Christ in and according to the new Covenant'.

In addition to laying down these broad principles, the tract
singled out one or two particular reforms which were to be made.
Central and local law courts were to be established, in which
lawyers would be dispensed with, for every man would be
allowed to plead his own cause. Tithes, customs and excise, and
other oppressive impositions were to be abolished; and impress-
ment of men for service in the forces was also to be done away
with.

In conclusion, the declaration proclaimed:

Being also thoroughly convinced of the Apostacy, Hypocrisie, Murders and Treason of Oliver Cromwell, the Head of this Apostasie, . . . we were encouraged, (though but a worm, yet not without hopes of being raised up, to be instrumentall to thrash the mountains) . . . to publish our principle to the world . . . that a Standard might be set up and displayed for all Saints that hunger after the Truth, that wait for Justice and Righteousnesse. . . . Wherefore, wee doe invite and call the Lord's People . . . to come in and be united with us in this Bottome, this Blessed Cause!

With regard to the actual force which was to carry out the revolt, the committee of ten decided that it should be divided into three companies, each of which was to have three officers— a Captain of the Front, a Captain of the Rear, and an Ensign-Bearer. Each of the companies was to be divided into files and half-files, the leaders of which were to be appointed by the company officers. One of the company captains was to be chosen by all the members of the force to be Chief Captain, or leader of the insurrection—and, as was to be expected, Venner was elected to this position of responsibility, but only after the conspirators had deliberated and 'sought the Lord till midnight'.

When all these arrangements had been made, Venner and his chief associates tried once again to draw others into the conspiracy. Their choice this time fell on the Baptists, many of whom were very close to the Fifth Monarchy Men in belief; but the Baptists declined to co-operate, because they judged that the time for revolt was not yet ripe.

Perseveringly, Venner then had an interview with Major-General Harrison, John Carew, John Rogers, and one or two other leading figures of the Fifth Monarchy sect. These brethren, however, proved as unfavourably disposed towards Venner's project as the Baptists had been. Carew declared that in his opinion Venner and his followers were 'not of a gospel spirit', and Rogers agreed with this judgement. What Harrison said is unrecorded; but he was as disinclined as Rogers and Carew to take part in what must have seemed, to his trained military mind, a hare-brained project doomed to failure from the start.

Nevertheless the fanatical Venner and his friends carried on stubbornly with their preparations, and by 23 March it was agreed that the revolt should begin on the night of Tuesday 7 April. The first step would be to meet at a suitable rendezvous, and then, if possible (to quote from the conspirators' own resolution), 'to fall upon a troop of horse and execute their officers and all others of the guards or private soldiers that shall oppose us, and take their horses to horse our men, because the Lord hath need; and to receive to mercy those of the soldiers that shall submit themselves'.

On Thursday 2 April the ten brethren who constituted the committee met to put in hand the final preparations. It was settled that Epping Forest should be the rendezvous, but that the rebels should assemble there on the night of 9 April, and not 7 April, as previously arranged. They were to come together in that part of the forest which was nearest to Chelmsford, because on Friday 10 April the printed declaration, *A Standard Set Up*, was to be proclaimed in the market-place there, and a call made to the people to stand up for Christ and their own liberties. Afterwards, the conspirators would march into Suffolk and Norfolk, because there they would find 'most Churches and Christians of this faith [i.e. Fifth Monarchists], and the country generally enclosed and soe most fitt for our purpose'.

At two final meetings on 5 April, however, dissensions broke out, and a number of the brethren refused to take any further part in the insurrection, and departed. Undeterred by this ominous last-minute secession, Venner and his comrades pressed on, and as the fateful day, 9 April, drew nearer, they were kept busy arranging for horses, arms, and ammunition to be available at various places in or near the City. It was from these places that the rebels were to make their way, in very small groups, so as to be as inconspicuous as possible, to the rendezvous in Epping Forest.

During these last few days Venner appears to have been able to hold meetings at his house in Catherine Lane near the Tower of London with complete impunity, perhaps because the Government wished its spies and informants to get as much knowledge of the plot as possible before stepping in to suppress it. At one such meeting on Sunday 5 April, William Ashton, a silk-weaver of Whitechapel, was admitted into 'church-membership' with Venner and his associates; and later, on Wednesday 8 April, Venner and another plotter called Craig came to Ashton's house and deposited arms and ammunition there, stating that they would return the next night to fetch away what they had hidden.

Arms and ammunition were deposited at other places too; and the plan, as finally agreed, was that late at night on 9 April the several groups of insurgents should make their way to a rendezvous at Mile End Green, and not in Epping Forest, as previously arranged. Here the revolt would be proclaimed, and action begin. The number of persons involved, after all the discussions, dissensions, and secessions, was very small—certainly less than a hundred—and Venner, fanatically oblivious to reality, seems to have hoped that his few chosen saints had only to assemble, unfurl the banner, and blow the clarion call, for multitudes to flock to their sides and join in the destruction of Babylon and the Beast.

What in fact happened, however, was harshly different from Venner's hopes and calculations. The Government's spies had learned about the plot in good time, and on being informed on the afternoon of 9 April that Venner and his own particular group had begun assembling at a house in Shoreditch, preparatory to their rendezvous at Mile End, the Government sent a troop of horse which surrounded the house. Twenty men, ready booted and spurred, were captured, including Venner himself; and a considerable store of arms and ammunition, as well as the insurgents' lion standard, and five hundred copies of their 'declaration', were seized. Other depots of the plotters were raided at the same time, including the meeting-place in Swan Alley, and further supplies of arms and ammunition were uncovered. In these places, however, the plotters (perhaps warned in time) avoided capture.

The reaction of the Government to all these events was, in the circumstances, astonishingly mild, and the insurgents appear to have been regarded as religious fanatics more deserving of pity than punishment. Venner himself was brought before Cromwell and the Council of State, and behaved in such an unrepentant and insolent manner that he was sent to the Tower. Here with his captured associates he was kept 'under strict and severe imprisonment', so the warrant ordered, but not brought to trial.

Only a few of the plotters had been captured on 9 April, and it was probably the remainder of them, some sixty in number, who, despite the loss of their leader, Venner, made a last desper-

ate attempt at the end of April to stage the revolt. This party too
was surprised and captured near Epping, and brought back on
horseback to London with their hands tied behind them. Like
their fellows taken three weeks earlier, they do not appear to have
been put on trial for their attempted revolt.

The Government, no doubt because it had heard of the
approaches made by Venner to Harrison and his friends, suspected the Major-General and Colonel Nathaniel Rich of complicity. Colonel Henry Danvers and Vice-Admiral Lawson, of
strong Fifth Monarchy leanings, also fell under suspicion; and
all four men were arrested and brought before the Council of
State.

No conclusive evidence could be brought against any of them,
however, and they were released. Despite this escape, Harrison
continued afterwards to consort with John Rogers, Christopher
Feake, and other well-known Fifth Monarchy Men at a Mr.
Daforme's house in Bartholomew Lane, near the Royal Exchange; and if information which came into Secretary Thurloe's
hands on 15 June 1657 was to be believed, they were at last, at
that late stage, ready to join in an insurrection against the Government. This was because they believed that the time had now
come when a revolt could take place in strict accordance with
the chronology of the biblical prophecies.

There can be no doubt that Harrison, Rogers, and Feake, like
Venner and the militant Fifth Monarchy Men, were influenced
by the recent trend of events in Whitehall. On 23 February 1657
Sir Christopher Pack had introduced a proposal in Parliament
that Cromwell should be asked to adopt the style and title of
King. This proposal undoubtedly reflected the desires of a good
many people, who were already hankering after the old traditional forms of government, particularly because of their dislike
of the military regime of the Major-Generals. After some weeks
of discussion Pack's proposals were embodied in a 'Humble
Petition and Advice' presented to Cromwell in the Banqueting
House, Whitehall, on 31 March. The Protector asked for time to
consider the proposals, and his answer, that he could not 'undertake that charge under this title' (i.e. of King), was given to Parliament on 4 April.

After further discussions between Protector and Parliament
an amended Petition and Advice was submitted for Cromwell's

approval on 25 May. This time he accepted the proposals, for the title of King had been dropped, though under the new dispensation Cromwell, as Lord Protector, had additional powers, such as the right to name his successor, which gave him a regal authority.

On 26 June 1657, comformably with his new status, Cromwell was re-installed with much pomp and ceremony as Lord Protector: 'Clothed in purple and ermine, invested with a Sword of State, and a sceptre of massy gold, he lacked nothing but a crown on his head, and the symbolic unction on his brow and breast, to make the ceremony seem a coronation.'[5]

It was these events, culminating in Cromwell's 'coronation', which aroused the hostility of the Fifth Monarchy Men to a new pitch of fury. John Rogers was moved to extreme indignation by this usurpation of the rights which should belong to King Jesus alone; and on 28 July 1657 his feelings were expressed in his book *Jegar-Sahadutha*.[6] The title of this was:

Jegar-Sahadutha:
an Oyled Pillar
Set up for Posterity
Against the present Wickednesses, Hypocrisies, Blasphemies, Persecutions and Cruelties of this Serpent Power (now up) in England (the Out-Street of the Beast).

Rogers' book had been written for the most part during his imprisonment in Carisbrooke Castle, and indeed the title-page carried the line 'From Carisbrook Castle in the third Year of my Captivity'; but its contents were very relevant, from the point of view of the Fifth Monarchy Men, to the situation in July 1657. In his introduction Rogers declared that the 'bloody BEAST (by a new Guize) hath acted again upon the stage of Great Britanny'; and he called for a revival of the spirit of the 'good old Puritans' which would maintain the cause of the martyred saints, and revenge their blood.

The call, he wrote in bold capitals, was to be 'UP AND

---

[5] Firth, *Last Years of the Protectorate* (London 1909), Vol. I, p. 200.

[6] 'Cairn of Witness'—the name given by Laban to the cairn of stones set up by Jacob as a testimony of the covenant the two had made (Genesis xxxi. 47).

DOING for the Lord Jesus the King of Saints'; and he added, 'it is now, within a year or two, as we shall show you!' As for 'this pittiful, pudlie, filthy, miery-clay-Government that is gotten up in Great Brittany', he declared, it was headed by Cromwell, 'this Bastard of Ashdod,[7] this illegitimate Monster'; and he called on his 'most dear and honoured brethren', Major-General Harrison, Mr. Courtney, Mr. Carew, Colonel Rich, Major-General Overton, Cornet Day, and Brother Feake, to 'make haste and march up, yea sally out most fiercely' upon the apostate and perfidious enemy of the saints.

Come come, Sirs, prepare your companies [he exhorted them] for King Jesus his Mount Zion musterday is at hand; His Magazine and Artillery, yea, His most excellent Mortar-pieces and batteries be ready; we wait only for the word from on High to fal on ... And then by the Grace of God, the proudest of them all shal know we are ingaged on life and death, to sink or swim, stand or fal with the Lord Jesus our Captain-General upon his Red Horse against the Beast's Government, so as neither to give nor take Quarter, but according to his Orders. Therefore, take the Alarum, my brethren, be up and ready! (p. 140.)

Despite the subversive language of Rogers' book he was left at liberty for the rest of 1657. In January 1658, however, the reports made to the Government by informants led to his arrest on a charge of inciting the people; and with his former fellow-prisoner, Hugh Courtney, he was consigned, on 3 February, to the Tower of London until further notice.

To add to Cromwell's difficulties at this time, he faced trouble once again with his Parliament, which had reassembled in January 1658. In accordance with one of the provisions of the *Humble Petition and Advice* the legislature consisted now of an Upper as well as a Lower House. Many of the Protector's staunchest supporters had been appointed to the new chamber, and so Cromwell's critics in the Lower House were left with a freer hand, and at once took advantage of it to call in question the powers not only of the new chamber, but of the Lord Protector as well.

This was too much for Cromwell; and, his patience exhausted,

---

[7] The city of the Philistines most execrated by the Jews, because the captured Ark of the Covenant had been installed there by the enemy.

he dissolved the Parliament on 4 February. 'I think it high time that an end be put to your sitting', he told the members, and added, 'I do declare to you here that I do dissolve this Parliament. Let God judge between you and me!'[8]

Discontent was now so prevalent that there was a real danger that the Royalists, aided and abetted by other malcontents like the Fifth Monarchy Men, might make a supreme effort to overthrow the regime. Cromwell viewed the state of affairs with such concern that on 12 March he requested the Lord Mayor and Aldermen of the City of London to come to Whitehall; and there he informed them of the dangers of the situation. This led the corporation to put in hand urgent measures to reorganize the City militia, and on 17 March to proclaim publicly, in an address, their loyalty to the Lord Protector and his Government.

This demonstration of support caused great anger amongst the Fifth Monarchy Men, and one of them, Cornet Wentworth Day, was reported by a Government informant on 18 March to have reviled the City fathers and the Lord Protector.

Cornett Daye in his prayer [the informant related] did envy [i.e. disparage] much the citty of London for joyneing with the great man at Whitehall with their lives and fortunes, and said it would be the cause of much blood; and in his sermon he had these expressions, that Oliver Cromwell was noe magistrate or governor; for he was not made soe by God nor man, unless the lord mayor and court of aldermen had made him soe. And also said that Oliver Cromwell was a jugler, and he would prove him soe by a substantiall witnesse . . . and that he deserved to be sawne in pieces![9]

Cornet Day pursued his diatribes at the notorious meeting-place in Swan Alley, Coleman Street, and there he referred to 'this treacherous city . . . that will live and die with this man of mischief!', and went on to castigate Cromwell once again as a 'juggler', or political trickster. At a meeting in Swan Alley on 1 April 1658 Cornet Day was in the company of Feake and another renowned Fifth Monarchy preacher, John Canne. The latter had served as chaplain to Major-General Overton when that officer had been Governor of Hull, and partly, no doubt, because

---

[8] Abbott, *The Writings and Speeches of Oliver Cromwell*, Vol. IV, p. 732.
[9] Thurloe, *State Papers*, Vol. VII, pp. 5–6.

of this association Canne became more deeply imbued than ever with Fifth Monarchy beliefs. In 1657 he had published *The Time of the End*, in which he interpreted the scriptural prophecies concerning the duration of the Fourth Monarchy, and the rise and downfall of the Little Horn, and left, as he stated in the title of his work, the application of his theories 'to the Wise'.

Both Feake and Rogers wrote introductions to Canne's book. Feake said that multitudes of people had been beguiled 'into a compliance with the interest of the Kingdom of the Beast'—but the saints had not been so deceived, for they had studied their Bible to good purpose. 'Although', he went on, 'we in our preachings and writings may to the present age seem audacious men, thus to meddle with these dark prophecies, yet the succeeding generations shall bless the Lord for raising up some before their times, to forewarn them to flee from the wrath that is to come!'

John Rogers styled his foreword 'An Epistolary Perambulation: or a word to everyone round the World', and in it he referred to Canne as 'this old sufferer and standard against the prelates and tyrants old and new', and as 'this aged brother and companion in tribulation'. He commended the reader to follow the author closely as 'he glides into the discovery of this *terra incognita*, the Little Horn'; and he ended by invoking woe on all who at the time of the end should be proved to have been 'involved with the Beast at this day'.

Canne stated that many of the Lord's worthies had spent much time in trying to ascertain the exact date when the saints ought to take action against Babylon. He himself had long and diligently examined the Scriptures, and particularly the prophecies, and thus he was now in a position to reveal the truth to his brethren. Without any doubt, Canne continued, the signs of the times showed that the Kingdom of God was nigh; and when the 'set time' fell due, the saints would publicly proclaim war against Babylon, and announce that the day of the vengeance of the Lord had come. Finally, in a very thinly veiled reference to the Cromwellian regime, Canne defined the 'Beast' as 'a State or Government set up by a few apostates, full of darknesse, great oppression exercised by reason the people have their power, laws and liberties taken from them'.

Such being the temper of Canne it was not surprising, perhaps, that when the news reached the authorities on 1 April

1658 that he was addressing a crowded congregation in Swan Alley, swift action was taken to bring the proceedings to a close. What happened is best recounted in a pamphlet subsequently issued by the saints themselves under the title:

A Narrative
Wherein is faithfully set forth the suffe-
rings of John Cann, Wentworth Day, John Clarke, John Belcher,
John Ricard, Robert Boggis, Petter Kidd, Richard Bry-
enton, and George Strange, called (as their
News Book saith) FIFT MO-
NARCHY MEN.
That is,
How Eight of them were taken in Coleman
street, Moneth second (called Aprill),[10] Day first, 1658, as they were
in the Solemn Worship of God, and by the Lord Mayor
sent Prisoners to the Counter in the Poultrey.[11]
Also
Of the Arraignment of Wentworth Day
and John Clarke, at the Sessions in the Old Bailey; and how
the rest after three weeks Imprisonment more
were Discharged in their Court.
Published by a Freind to the Prisoners and the Good Old
Cause they suffered for.

On 1 April, the narrative began, many of the Lord's People had assembled in Swan Alley in Coleman Street, 'a public place where Saints have met many years', and 'old Brother Cann was then in the Pulpit, and had read a place of Scripture, but spoken nothing to it'. At this moment officers of the City Marshal burst into the meeting-place, and one of them pulled Canne down from the pulpit, and then 'hurled him over the benches or forms in a very barbarous manner'.

The Lord Mayor himself was waiting outside, on horseback, attended by a sheriff, and Canne was first brought before him, and then taken to the Counter. Seven members of the congregation who had complained about the violence with which Canne had been handled were also sent to the Counter, where they were

---

[10] Under the old style the year began in March.
[11] The Counters were prisons under the control of the sheriffs. The Counter in the Poultry (south of Grocers' Hall in Cheap Ward) was demolished in 1815.

thrust into a 'cold stinking hole'; and they were kept there without beds till the following day, when all the prisoners came before the Lord Mayor for questioning.

Canne was the first to be dealt with, and the Lord Mayor
began by asking him what he thought of the present Government. Canne replied candidly that he was not satisfied with it,
and added: 'If you send me to the Protector, I shall tell him
what I think concerning this Government. For I have a great
deal to say to his face, if in such a way as this I may be brought
before him. But', he ended reprovingly to the Lord Mayor, 'for
you, Sir, this is not our business now!'

At this Canne was taken away and Cornet Wentworth Day
brought in. The Lord Mayor put the same question to him, only
to be given an even more forthright reply. Day declared that if he
could be brought face to face with Cromwell, he would prove
the latter 'a jugler by his own confession'. So that there should
be no doubt about this undertaking, Day went to the trouble
of writing it down on a piece of paper which he left with the Lord
Mayor, after which he too was led away.

Brother Clarke, who was next questioned, replied sturdily that
in his opinion the Government was 'not of God', and he proceeded to quote the Scriptures at length to prove this. By this
time, however, the Lord Mayor had grown impatient; so all the
prisoners (save Brother Ricard who against his own wishes was
bailed out by his master) were sent back to the Counter.

After three weeks Wentworth Day, incriminated by the piece
of paper which he had left with the Lord Mayor, was put on trial
for having called Oliver Cromwell, the Lord Protector, a juggler.
Day denied that the court had any competence to try him, for, he
asserted, the members were not men who feared God, or men of
truth. He was, moreover, convinced, he said, that in their own
hearts they too realized that Cromwell was a juggler; but that
they did not say so openly, because 'self-interest had blinded
them'.

Not surprisingly, at this point the officers of the court received
instructions to remove the recalcitrant prisoner, and he was
forcibly led away from the bar. He was brought back into court
the next day, however, and asked whether he pleaded guilty or
not. He refused to plead at all; and instead harangued the
court, alleging that the Lord Mayor had imprisoned him on false

grounds, and that the warrant under which he had been detained 'had no more law in it than a horse'. He expected 'satisfaction' for this unlawful treatment, he said; and without pausing to find out whether he had any hopes of getting it, he proceeded to damage his chances irretrievably. For, he roundly told the court, they sat not as judges, but as murderers; and then, with sublime optimism, Day requested leave to quote the Scriptures to prove his assertion. When permission was refused, he announced loudly that he wanted to have nothing more to do with the court, since 'they would not take the word of God for their rule and guide'. Never ceasing in his tirade, he had just added that he wondered that they were not ashamed to read such a pack of lies against him, when the court officers descended on him once again, and took him away, still vehemently protesting.

With exemplary patience the court decided to give him a third chance; and he was accordingly brought to the bar again on 24 April. This time he had support in the persons of Christopher Feake and John Rogers, the latter of whom had been released from his detention in the Tower of London (where he had been consigned on 3 February 1658) a few days previously.

Rogers stood at Day's side, and the irrepressibly optimistic Cornet asked leave 'to read a Scripture'. Lord Chief Justice Glyn said that he could not be allowed to do this. This reply made Day lose his temper, and he cried out furiously that the judge was a traitor who had betrayed his trust and his country. Because of this gross contempt Day was immediately removed from court; but after a short adjournment he was brought back again. Absolutely incorrigible, he at once began to read out an impeachment for high treason against Lord Chief Justice Glyn; and when he was forcibly made to desist from this, he quickly changed his ground, and declared that he now had twelve witnesses to prove that Cromwell was a juggler. He desired, therefore, that those persons might be brought to court so that their testimony could be heard.

Day had tried the patience of the court for too long, however; his request was disregarded, and without any more formalities he was fined £500 and given a year's imprisonment as well, with the warning that he would be released after the expiration of his sentence only if he gave security for his good behaviour in the future.

This judgement served only to confirm Day in his conviction
that he was a martyr; and with a characteristically wilful mis-
representation of the recent proceedings, he proclaimed to the
court that he found it very strange that he should be sentenced
before he had had a chance to state his case; and he continued in
the same strain until, for the last time, he was removed from the
court.

The other accused were tried shortly afterwards, and were all
discharged on 25 April save Brother Clarke, who was fined for
a contempt of court, and also sentenced to six months' imprisonment. Even though all the brethren but two had been released,
'Old Brother Cann' was not content to depart quietly. After
the acquittal had been announced, he asked that he might have
liberty to speak a few words. The Lord Mayor told him curtly
that he had been acquitted, and that that was enough. 'I pray
you, Sir,' replied Canne, 'give me the liberty which the heathen
gave Paul, when he was before them. . . .'

The implied comparison proved the last straw for the sorely-
tried Lord Mayor; and he gave order that Canne and his
brethren should be removed from the court-room, and made to
depart.

It was the humourless, vociferous fanaticism of the Fifth Monarchy Men which turned from them many people who might
otherwise, given the credulity of the age, have found their millenarian doctrines satisfying. As it was, their extravagances
brought them into disrepute with ordinary folk. Thus John
Evelyn recorded in his diary on 6 August 1657: 'Our Viccar,
18 Joh. 36,[12] declaiming at the folly of a sort of Enthusiasts and
desperat Zealots, cald the fift Monarchy-men, pretending to set
up the Kingdom of Christ with the Sword; to this passe was this
age arrivd, when we had no King in Israel!'

Soon, however, there was to be once more a 'King in Israel'.
The restoration of the Stuarts was approaching; and the Fifth
Monarchy Men were destined to find that the Government of
Charles II, unlike the understanding, patient, and tolerant
Cromwell, would deal with the saints in merciless fashion.

---

[12] 'Jesus answered, [to Pilate] My Kingdom is not of this
world. . . .'

7

BLOOD WILL HAVE BLOOD

THE Parliament which Cromwell dissolved on 4 February 1658 was his last. Worn out by the cares and disappointments of office, troubled continuously by reports of plots against his regime and his life, deeply distressed by the death of his favourite daughter on 6 August, the Protector fell a prey to illness, his condition grew rapidly worse, and on 3 September 1658, the anniversary of his great victories at Dunbar and Worcester, he died.

The Fifth Monarchy Men kept themselves informed of the worsening of Cromwell's condition, and seem to have had hopes of arranging a *coup d'état* on his death, with Major-Generals Lambert and Harrison as leaders. When it was clear that Cromwell had only a few more hours to live, they sent out emissaries to various parts of the country, probably with details of the proposed plan; but nothing came of it, and Richard Cromwell succeeded his father without incident.

On his death-bed Cromwell had nominated Richard, his third son, as his successor, and a new Parliament which assembled on 27 January 1659 confirmed this. Sir Henry Vane was returned as a member of this Parliament, and he and a number of other Republicans, though unable to prevent the confirmation of Richard's title, remained firmly opposed to him. For other reasons too, Richard's position was precarious in the extreme. He lacked his father's strength of character and will to defend his position and authority, and this proved fatal in the troubled, almost chaotic conditions which soon prevailed. Like Oliver's, Richard's regime depended on the loyalty and support of the Army; but Richard, a civilian, did not command the respect enjoyed by Oliver, the great parliamentary general. Soon, therefore, a section of the Army, headed by Lieutenant-General Fleetwood, who had married Richard's sister, Bridget, was manoeuvring to make the Army independent of the Protector, and a State within the State.

Tired and disillusioned by the conflict, Richard dissolved

Parliament on 22 April 1659; but the Army now decided that some kind of legislature was necesssry after all, to give a semblance of constitutional propriety to the situation. In this extremity it was decided to recall the old Rump, and on 7 May forty-two members dutifully followed Speaker Lenthall into the chamber. The Rump agreed that in the future the country should be a Commonwealth, without a Protector and a Second Chamber; and on 25 May Richard accepted this new settlement and retired thankfully to Hampton Court and the peaceful private life which he had never ceased to yearn for.

The Rump appointed a Council of State and a Committee of Public Safety, and with the aid of these it tried to govern the country. Still resolutely refusing to admit the members excluded by Pride's Purge, the Rump carried on its deliberations in conditions of increasing uncertainty. A letter written from London on 3 June 1659 described the situation in the country at this time:

The confusions here are so great [the writer, a Major Wood, said] that it is not to be credited; the Chaos was a perfection in comparison of our order and government; the parties are like so many floating islands, sometimes joining and appearing like a continent, when the next flood or ebb separates them, that it can hardly be known where they will be next.... Three days since about five thousand of the Fifth Monarchy Men met at Horsham in Sussex, and dispersed after eight hours consultation. There are two or three thousand of them well-armed, and officers appointed to every thousand and every hundred; Harrison is their general and Vane their Chancellor; they say they must begin at the altar, and with fire and sword prepare the coming of Christ. We daily expect a massacre; it was deferred this week, and is to be performed upon Tuesday night next.[1]

Major Wood seems merely to have been repeating some of the wild rumours about the Fifth Monarchy Men which were prevalent at this time, for three days later a broadsheet was published and circulated in London, which also drew attention to an alleged Fifth Monarchy plot. The contents of this publication began as follows: 'An Alarum to the City and Souldiery, God grant they may not neglect it'; and it went on to warn against a

---

[1] *Clarendon State Papers* (Oxford 1767–86), Vol. III, p. 479.

An Alarum to the City and Souldiery,

God grant. they may not neglect it.

Gentlemen, and fellow Souldiers,

AT this time, when our Ruine and Deſtruction is upon us, there is no place for many words. The Fifth Monarchy men are Arm'd, Officer'd, and every way in a Readineſs, upon the word given them, to ſurpriſe and ſuppreſs the Army, to Fire the City, and to Maſſacre all conſiderable People of all ſorts, whom they ſuſpect averſe to what they impiouſly deſigned. *Feake* hath lately ⸱ them the Alarum in Print: Sir *Henry Vane* is Chief in the Deſign, and lately ſaid in confidence to a Friend, This Army was any way to be ſuppreſs'd; for otherwiſe, they ſhould not be permitted to ſit long. The Parliaments new *Militia*, and their Liſtings in ſeveral Counties, is in order to no other Deſign. If God gives you not eyes to ſee the deſtruction that is even at your dores, or if you ſee it, you want hearts and courage to prevent it, it then ſeems the Decree is gone out againſt you. You have your Warning, and we have done our Duties. Beware *Tueſday* next; we ſay, Beware. *June 6. 1659.*

plot by the Fifth Monarchy Men to set fire to the City of London and carry out a massacre of prominent people.

Though the rumoured rising of the Fifth Monarchy Men did not take place, the spokesmen of the sect were not reticent in putting forward their views. The reversion to a Commonwealth had revived their hopes that the oft-deferred reign of the saints might now at last be about to begin; and, as usual, much advice was offered in tracts and pamphlets to hasten this consummation.

On 2 May Christopher Feake had published: 'A Beam of Light shining In the midst of much Darkness and Confusion'.

In this tract Feake recapitulated the history of events in England since the Civil War, and declared that the cause of the saints had been betrayed. His conclusion was that 'the interest of the real Fifth Kingdom-men, in this day' was to wait together:

in one spirit to become a *peculiar people* (or as it were, a *Nation in the midst of the Nation*), waiting for the word of command from their leader, *to execute the vengeance written against Babylon,* for being *drunk with the bloud of the Saints.* . . . Courage! Courage, dear Hearts! [Feake exhorted his readers] *The Great Whore which hath corrupted the earth with her fornications, and hath shed the bloud of the Saints of the Most High . . . is to be stript naked, is to be made desolate!*

Feake ended on a note of urgency: 'You are invited to be in a readinesse, and at an hours warning, to *plead and to promote this blessed businesse!*'

On 10 May, three days after the reassembly of the Rump, John Canne, too, had been active, and had published: 'A Seasonable Word to the Parliament-Men To take with them when they go into the House'.

Canne declared that the reassembly of the Rump was due to 'a wonderful hand of Providence', and that great issues were now at stake. 'The Lord by you', he said to the members, 'either intends to heal the great breaches of this miserable Nation, and thereby make your memories blessed; or to bring us yet lower, and make our wounds greater and deeper, and that by you.'

Canne concluded that the Rump must 'give Jesus Christ his rights'—and that if they did this, the Parliament would prove a blessing to the nation. It must be said that from Canne's point of view, the recalled Rump began very promisingly. He himself was appointed to the position of official news-writer, and from mid-

May to mid-August 1659 he edited the two Government news-papers, the *Mercurius Politicus,* and the *Publick Intelligencer.* Moreover, that friend and supporter of the saints' cause, Sir Henry Vane, was made a member of both the Council of State and the Committee of Public Safety, so that Parliament did indeed seem intent on giving Jesus Christ his rights.

These early signs of grace were not, however, followed by others, and Parliament and the saints soon fell out over the old problem of tithes. The Fifth Monarchy Men, true to their anti-Establishment principles, wished these at last to be abolished. However Parliament showed a firmer grasp of reality, and on 14 June resolved that until a better means of encouraging and maintaining a godly, learned ministry could be devised, tithes were to remain.

Disagreement over this and other matters was stilled for the time being by the outbreak of a Royalist insurrection in Cheshire under Sir George Booth. In face of this common danger Parliament and Fifth Monarchy Men co-operated. While Major-General Lambert at the head of the regular forces was dealing with Booth, three volunteer regiments were hastily formed, the command of which was given to Sir Henry Vane; and Fifth Monarchy Men were among the many anti-Royalists who enrolled in these reserve formations.

Booth's rising was suppressed on 19 August, and Parliament now felt free to consider the question of the future government of the country. The Fifth Monarchy Men once more felt their hopes rising, and again presented their views in a number of pamphlets. On 23 August 1659 specific proposals were set down in a tract entitled:

The Fifth Monarchy,
or
Kingdom of Christ
In Opposition to the
Beasts
Asserted. . . .
With a short application, and some
brief proposals grounded on Scripture in
order to a lasting Settlement in this hour
of Distraction; the Foundations being
out of course.

In this tract the anonymous author or authors repeated the traditional Fifth Monarchy propositions. Christ Jesus, they said, should be publicly proclaimed the only Lord and King of the country; and his laws, as found in the Old and New Testaments, should be made the laws of the nation, in place of the 'heathenish, tyrannous and popish laws' which were still in force. As for Church affairs, a thorough reformation was necessary, involving the extirpation of all existing ecclesiastical offices, and such long-standing abuses as tithes.

John Rogers, who like his old companion in misfortune, Christopher Feake, could never refrain from giving advice on the advancement of Christ's Kingdom, published on 20 September 1659, 'A Christian Concertation with Mr. Prin, Mr. Baxter, Mr. Harrington, For the True Cause of the Commonwealth'.

In this tract Rogers, for once, was on the side of the Government; and it is not uncharitable to suppose that this change of attitude was due, partly at least, to the fact that Parliament had just appointed him chaplain of one of the regiments under Lambert's command. He thereupon engaged in spirited controversy with critics of the Government, among them the redoubtable William Prynne, the Puritan hero who had earned undying fame through having had both his ears cut off in 1634 because he allegedly libelled Henrietta Maria, wife of Charles I.

Rogers tried to refute aspersions which Prynne, Baxter, and Harrington had lately cast upon Parliament and the Council of State; and after dealing with what he called 'the venome and vilification of their pens', he addressed a postscript to 'The Parliament of the Commonwealth now returned to the great exercise of the Supreme Trust'. With commendable optimism, in view of the melancholy precedent set by Barebone's Parliament, Rogers declared he was certain that 'theocratic government' would, with God's blessing, 'prove such a settlement as shall satisfie all parties and honest interests in the Commonwealth'; and in conclusion he proclaimed: 'For which cause and the Commonwealth . . . I do profess for one (amongst the thousands of Israel) I am ready, hearty and resolved (with the Lord's grace and assistance) to live or to dy!'

The Rump, however, proved unwilling to adopt any of the proposals put forward by Rogers and the other Fifth Monarchy pamphleteers, and its indecision encouraged Major-General

Lambert to take action. On 13 October 1659 he led his men to London, and as a result the Rump's sessions were once more suspended. By now the country was tired of *coups d'état*, or attempted *coups d'état*, and after three months of uncertainty the Rump was restored on 26 December. General Monk in Scotland, sensing the widespread discontent, marched with his troops from that country at the beginning of January 1660, and entered London on 3 February.

The Rump welcomed him as a deliverer; but Monk was determined to get a better basis for the restoration of the Stuarts which more and more seemed to be the only way out of the prevailing uncertainty and developing chaos. Accordingly, on 21 February the members who had been excluded by Pride's Purge in December 1648 were readmitted to Parliament; and this enlarged Rump agreed that its session should end, and that there should be fresh elections for a new Parliament to meet on 25 April 1660.

Monk, now certain that the restoration of the Stuarts was the only alternative to anarchy, sent emissaries to the exiled Charles in Holland, and received from him in the 'Declaration of Breda' an assurance that pardon would be extended to all, save such persons as Parliament should except, who had opposed the King. The Declaration of Breda was submitted to the new Parliament, called the 'Convention Parliament', which met on 25 April and the members then voted for the restoration of the monarchy, and begged Charles to return and assume the royal office as soon as possible. He was proclaimed in London on 8 May; and on 29 May, his birthday, he entered London amid scenes of great rejoicing.

During the troubled uncertain weeks which preceded the restoration of Charles II the Fifth Monarchy Men seem to have behaved passively, accepting what was to them a disastrous turn of events with unaccustomed meek resignation—almost as if, like most of their fellow-countrymen, they were so tired of political convulsions that they wanted stability at any cost.

Meanwhile the Convention Parliament was busy preparing to exact vengeance on the regicides, amongst whom were two prominent Fifth Monarchy Men, Major-General Harrison and John Carew. Both of these had had ample chance to escape the wrath to come, but both had declined to do so. Carew had lived

in retirement in Cornwall since his release in 1656 from imprisonment in Pendennis Castle; and though both he and Harrison were suspected of being involved in plots against the
Protectorate in 1658, and had been taken into custody again,
they were both released, and went once again into retirement.

Harrison was arrested at his house in Newcastle-under-Lyme
at the end of April 1660, and with Carew, who had been
brought from Cornwall, was committed to the Tower of London.
They were later transferred to Newgate Prison with other regicides, and on 10 October 1660 were brought to the Sessions
House in the Old Bailey to hear the indictment against them.

When Harrison was asked if he pleaded guilty or not guilty,
he complained that he had been kept a close prisoner for three
months, that he had not been allowed to see anybody, and
that he had not known until nine o'clock the previous evening
that his trial was soon to begin. Nevertheless, after much argument he agreed to plead not guilty; but then another argument
developed when he was asked how he wished to be tried. Instead
of answering, as required, 'By God and the country', Harrison
said, 'According to the Laws of the Lord.' A long dispute ensued;
and then once again, reluctantly, Harrison gave way and consented to use the traditional form of words.

His trial, the first in the series, began on 11 October, and the
prosecutor, Sir Heneage Finch, the Solicitor-General, in his
speech to the jury, called Harrison 'the conductor, leader and
captain' of all the proceedings taken against King Charles. In
his defence Harrison argued that the trial and execution of the
King had been carried out in the name of, and with the authority
of Parliament. Hence, Harrison said, the present court had no
jurisdiction to try him, and the only court which could was the
High Court of Parliament itself.

The prosecution's answer to this was that Parliament consisted of King, Lords, and Commons; and that apart from the
fact that the King and the House of Lords had taken no part in
condemning and executing the King, the House of Commons
itself had previously been unlawfully reduced in number by
Pride's Purge. On the plea of justification by parliamentary
authority Harrison was therefore overruled; and he was then
asked: 'Have you anything else to offer?'

In reply he stated that he had proceeded against King

Charles only because the monarch had set up his standard against the people of England, and had thus caused the blood of many Englishmen to be shed. The court was scandalized to hear this; and Sir Edward Turner, attorney to the Duke of York, cried out with unctuous indignation: 'My Lords, this man hath the plague all over him; it is pity any should stand near him, for he will infect them. Let us say to him, as they used to write over an house infected, "The Lord Have mercy upon him"; and so let the officer take him away!'

Harrison persisted in his claim that what he had done he had done by 'the Supreme Authority', and that the court could not call him to question. Finally, therefore, Sir Orlando Bridgman, Lord Chief Baron of the Court of the Exchequer, and President of the commission appointed to try the regicides, addressed the jury. He told them that the evidence against the prisoner was so clear that there was no need for them to retire to consider their verdict. The jurymen thereupon consulted dutifully among themselves for a brief while, and then returned a unanimous verdict of guilty.

The clerk now turned to Harrison and asked him: 'What hast thou to say for thyself why judgement should not pass against thee, to die according to law?'

Harrison, knowing that his case was hopeless, replied: 'I have nothing further to say, because the court have not seen meet to hear what was in my heart to speak. I submit to it.'

The crier then made proclamation for silence in court, and the Lord Chief Baron passed sentence on the prisoner.

The judgement of this court is, and the court doth award that you be led back to the place from whence you came, and from thence to be drawn upon an hurdle to the place of execution, and there you shall be hanged by the neck, and being alive, shall be cut down, and your privy members to be cut off, your entrails to be taken out of your body, and (you living) the same to be burnt before your eyes; and your head to be cut off, your body to be divided into four quarters, to be disposed of at the pleasure of the King's Majesty; and the Lord have mercy upon your soul!

Harrison's answer to these gruesome words was serene. 'Whom men have judged', he declared, 'God doth not condemn. Blessed be the name of the Lord!' He maintained this courageous attitude as he was led away through the jostling crowd who

shouted abuse at him outside the court. 'Good is the Lord for all
this!' Harrison cried; 'I have no reason to be ashamed of the
cause I have been engaged in!'

Back at Newgate, he was incarcerated in a dungeon and
chained by the feet to a wall. Here too his brave demeanour
astonished and impressed the people who came into contact with
him. A woman who had been sent down to tidy up the dungeon
was asked what she thought of the Major-General; and she
replied that she did not know what he had done to deserve to be
in Newgate—but she was sure he was a good man, for he was
full of God.

On the morning of Saturday 13 October, the date fixed for
the execution, the sheriff came to Harrison's dungeon and told
him that he must leave for the scaffold in half an hour's time.
Harrison employed the respite in saying farewell to his wife and
his friends. He gave his Bible to his wife; and then, turning to
his friends, he asked them to manifest their love for him by being
tender and kind to her.

By now the half-hour's grace was over, and the sheriff and his
officers reappeared. Harrison was bound with ropes around his
arms and shoulders, and then taken to the hurdle or sledge on
which, in accordance with custom, he was to be dragged to the
scaffold. 'Which way must I sit?' he asked; adding, with a
pathetic courage, 'For I am not acquainted with this!'

About nine o'clock he was drawn away; and according to the
testimony of eye-witnesses, he went 'with a sweet smiling coun-
tenance, with his eyes and hands lifted up to heaven, his coun-
tenance never changing all the way'.

As he was pulled along towards Charing Cross, he cried out
several times in a loud voice to the spectators who lined the route:
'I go to suffer upon the account of a most glorious cause that
ever was in the world!'

Amidst the jeers which these protestations of his faith evoked,
he heard one citizen inquire derisively: 'And now—where is your
good old cause?'

Smiling cheerfully, Harrison indicated his breast, and shouted
back: 'Here it is! And I am going to seal it with my blood!'

At the gallows by Charing Cross, after Harrison had been
taken from the sledge, the hangman came up to him and asked
his forgiveness for what he was about to do.

'I do forgive thee, with all my heart!' Harrison said, and added: 'Alas, poor man! Thou dost it ignorantly; the Lord grant that this sin may not be laid to thy charge!'

Then, impulsively putting his hand in his pocket, with a valedictory gesture on the scaffold that was not uncommon in those times, he gave the hangman all the money he had; and after embracing his servant in a last farewell, he mounted the steps to the gallows. Here, in accordance with tradition, he was allowed to address the crowd.

Gentlemen, [he said] I will speak something of the work God had in hand in our days. Many of you have been witnesses of the Finger of God, that hath been seen amongst us of late years, in the deliverance of his people from their oppressors; and in bringing to judgement those that were guilty of the precious blood of the dear servants of the Lord.... In which work I with others was engaged, for the which I do from my soul bless the name of God, who out of the exceeding riches of His Grace, accounted me worthy to be instrumental in so glorious a work. And though I am wrongfully charged with murder and bloodshed, yet I must tell you I have kept a good conscience, both towards God and towards Man. I never had malice against any man; neither did I act maliciously towards any person, but as I judged them to be enemies to God and his people. The Lord is my witness that I have done what I did out of the sincerity of my heart to the Lord ... my aim in all my proceedings was the glory of God, and the good of His People, and the welfare of the whole Commonwealth!

At this point in his speech, no doubt because he was overcome by emotion, Harrison's legs and arms began to tremble; and lest this should be wrongly interpreted by the crowd, he went on:

Gentlemen, by reason of some scoffing that I doe hear, I judge that some do think I am afraid to die, by the shaking I have in my hands and knees. I tell you, no, but it is by reason of much blood I have lost in the wars, and many wounds I have received in my body, which caused this shaking and weakness, in my nerves. I have had it these twelve years ... If I had been minded to have run away [he continued], I might have had many opportunities; but being so clear in the Thing, I durst not turn my back nor step a foot out of the way, by reason I had been engaged in the service of so glorious and great a God—

The sheriff now reminded him that the time allotted to him

was nearly over; so Harrison prayed, with tears in his eyes, and ended bravely with the words:

God hath covered my head many times in the day of battle; by God I have leaped over a wall; by God I have run through a troop; and by my God I will go through this death, and He will make it easy to me. Now into thy hands, O Lord Jesus, I commend my Spirit![2]

The execution was carried out in conformity with all the grisly rites which the law demanded, with one or two gratuitously sadistic additions. For example, Harrison was hanged with his face looking down Whitehall in the direction of the Banqueting House, outside which Charles I had been executed; and with another such flourish, his head was afterwards placed on a pole set on top of the south-east end of Westminster Hall.

Pepys witnessed the whole horrible business, and left a matter-of-fact account of it in his diary, under the date 13 October 1660.

I went out to Charing Cross, to see Major-General Harrison hanged, drawn and quartered; which was done there, he looking as cheerful as any man could do in that condition. He was presently cut down, and his head and heart shown to the people, at which there was great shouts of joy. It is said, that he said that he was sure to come shortly at the right hand of Christ to judge them that had now judged him; and that his wife do expect his coming again. Thus it was my chance to see the King beheaded in White Hall, and to see the first blood shed in revenge for the King at Charing Cross.

In Harrison the Fifth Monarchists lost one of their more likeable and level-headed brethren. A contemporary said of him that he was 'naturally of such a vivacity, hilarity and alacrity as another man hath when he hath drunken a cup too much';[3] and with this worldly demeanour worldly vanities were associated. He wore his hair long and curled like a cavalier, and had a love of finery and ostentation and an addiction to the acquisition of worldly goods which assorted oddly with his otherwise sternly puritanical nature.

---

[2] *The Indictment, Arraignment, Tryal and Judgment at large of Twenty-Nine Regicides* (1739), p. 222.

[3] Baxter, *Reliquiae Baxterianae* (London 1696), Part I, p. 57.

MAJOR GEN.^L HARRISON,

Executed at Charing Cross. 1660.

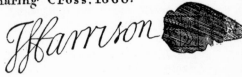

His career and above all his end testified, however, to qualities which more than made up for his weaknesses. His outstanding characteristic, apart from his great endowment of courage, was fidelity to the cause he believed in. He sacrificed for the cause of the saints what would otherwise have been, no doubt, an outstanding career; and he lavished his loyalty without reserve upon a millenarian delusion. 'He was a man of great heat and resolution, fixed in his principles', wrote a contemporary, Bishop Burnet;[4] and a later historian has most aptly summed him up as:

a man born to lead forlorn hopes and die for lost causes, who did both even to the admiration of his enemies. Unselfish in his own aims, he swayed others by his devotion and zeal. But he was fitter to command the left-wing in the battle of Armageddon than to take any part in the government of earthly states.[5]

John Carew, the other leading Fifth Monarchist who had taken part in the King's trial, pleaded, like Harrison, not guilty to the charge of high treason, and again like Harrison argued that the trial and execution of the King had been perfectly legal, having been carried out by authority of Parliament, and in accordance with God's holy and righteous laws. Inevitably, Carew was found guilty, condemned to the same barbarous death as had been meted out to Harrison; and on 15 October he went to his end with the same courage that Harrison had shown.

With two prominent exponents of millenarianism executed, and with a general reaction against the excesses of Puritanism in full swing, it might well seem that after the Restoration little was to be feared from the Fifth Monarchy Men. This was not so, however. Thomas Venner, the arch-fanatic, was waiting impatiently in the wings; and soon he was to descend once again on his stage, the City of London, to play the chief part in a sensational and bloody finale.

---

[4] Burnet, *History of His Own Time* (Oxford 1823), Vol. I, p. 275.
[5] Firth, *Oliver Cromwell* (Oxford 1958), p. 321.

8

A BLOW FOR KING JESUS

THOMAS VENNER and his leading associates had been incarcerated in the Tower of London on 9 April 1657 after their abortive plot against the Protectorate. For some reason or other they were never brought to trial, and at the end of February 1659 they were released by an act of clemency of the new regime of Richard Cromwell. Completely undeterred by their long spell of imprisonment they at once resumed their Fifth Monarchy activities at the meeting-place in Swan Alley, Coleman Street, and elsewhere.

The shifting, kaleidoscopic pattern of events which followed the death of Oliver Cromwell induced them to hope that the consummation for which they so devoutly prayed, the rule of the saints, might be inaugurated by peaceful means through a new Parliament of the righteous. When this hope was dissipated, however, and the restoration of the monarchy took place, Venner and a small band of fanatical followers planned another armed insurrection.

Little information has survived about the preparations made for this revolt; but, as in 1657, a printed tract was produced for distribution, and from this some idea of the aims of the conspirators can be gained. The tract was headed: 'A Door of Hope or A Call and Declaration for the gathering together of the first ripe Fruits unto the Standard of our Lord KING JESUS'.

The tract declared that Charles Stuart, the son of 'that murtherer' Charles I, had been proclaimed King, but that his throne of iniquity was built on the blood of precious saints and martyrs. The 'sweet harmony and agreement of the Prophecies', the 'wonderful, undeniable signs of the times', and, above all, the fact that Venner and his associates had manifestly been 'miraculously cut out and preserved' for the work to be done, had mightily awakened them and stirred them up, so that the fire which had long been hidden under their ashes would soon break out into flame.

They were resolved, therefore, 'to gird on a sword for Christ', to 'become souldiers in the Lamb's Army, abhorring mercenary principles and interests', and to drive out the Lord's enemies from the country. That, however, would not be the end of the work. The tract continued:

We are not purposed when the Lord shall have driven forth our enemies here in these Nations, and when we shall in a holy triumph have led our captivity captive, to sit down under our vines and figg trees, but to go on to France, Spain, Germany and Rome, to destroy the beast and whore, to burn her flesh with fire, to throw her down with violence as a millstone into the sea ... to bring not only these, but all the nations to the subjection of Christ.

The writers of the tract next defined the Kingdom of Christ which they desired to set up as: 'A well-ordered Common-wealth, ruled by the best of men, of found principles, of known integrity, haters of bribes and covetousnesse', and having the word of God as their rule. In conformity with the pattern of the 1657 manifesto, *A Standard Set Up*, a list of miscellaneous re-forms to be carried out followed the enunciation of the general principle. Justice was to be 'equally administered between man and man, without respect to poor or rich, bond or free'; theft would no longer be punishable by death; permission would no longer be given to export fuller's earth, unwrought leather, and other commodities to foreign parts lest industry at home be harmed and the workers impoverished; and finally the nation's stock of timber was to be conserved and increased.

The manifesto now turned to King Charles II, whom it described as 'a profest enemy, a rebel and traytor to Christ'; and then declared that there was a great design afoot to conquer England for Popery once again. Therefore, the writers asserted, they had not only a sufficient reason from Scripture for rebellion, but another justification also in that the liberties of themselves and their families were threatened by the 'beastly crew' in power. To take up the sword against them was, in fact, the only remedy left.

In a final declaration of purpose which followed, the writers stated that they would abolish the 'antichristian magistracy,

ministry, tythes, etc.', and would raze and root them out, so that
all yokes and oppressions, both civil and spiritual, should be removed from the necks of the people. They therefore called on
all followers of Christ to join in their revolt, which, after elaborate calculations, they proved must take place without delay to
be in conformity with the chronology of the biblical prophecies.

The Government had early warning that seditious activities
were going on, for in December 1660 reports had come in that
the Fifth Monarchy Men were planning another insurrection.
One of Venner's accomplices met an old acquaintance, an ex-
soldier named Hall, in a London tavern; and after a bout of
drinking had loosened his tongue, he informed Hall that a great
enterprise was in hand for the good of the well-affected in the
nation. On being asked what the enterprise was, the Fifth Monarchy Man divulged, with drunken frankness: 'We'll pull
Charles out of his throne, with the rest of the family, and have
the blood of Monk, and settle a Free State again, as it was in the
Little [Barebone's] Parliament, for the Saints must reign!'[1]

As soon as he was able to, Hall went to the nearest Justice of
the Peace and disclosed what he had been told in the tavern.
Afterwards, he was taken to Whitehall where he informed King
Charles himself of what the Fifth Monarchy Man had said. As
a result many houses were searched, and a number of suspects were
arrested, including Major-General Overton and Quartermaster-General Courtney, as well as various other discontented
Army officers.

Strangely, however, the actual plotters, Venner and his comrades, managed to escape detection; and brooking delay no
longer, decided to begin their desperate venture on 6 January
1661. This was the Feast of the Epiphany, and may have been
chosen by Venner because of its religious significance. Contemporaries believed, however, that the day was selected because the
insurgents hoped to find the City watchmen and guards still
drunk and incapacitated after the traditional Twelfth Night
festivities.[2]

Venner and his accomplices, some fifty in number, left their
meeting-place in Swan Alley, and made their way to St. Paul's,

---

[1] Pagitt, *Heresiography* (London 1662), p. 225.
[2] *Calendar of State Papers Venetian*, 21 January 1661.

where they arrived as darkness set in. They found the doors locked; and after they had tried in vain to get the keys, they broke open a door and entered the cathedral. Their purpose appears to have been to use the building as a fortress for a time, but after some consideration they decided that it would not be suitable. While they were still deliberating, one of the band who had been posted outside as a sentry challenged a passer-by, and asked him whom he was for. On receiving the reply 'King Charles!' the sentry cried out that *he* was for King Jesus—and then shot the unfortunate passer-by dead.

This incident, being reported to the City authorities, caused them to call out the citizen militia, the train-bands, under the Lord Mayor himself. However these hastily-assembled forces were unable to prevent the retreat of Venner and his men, who marched first to Bishopsgate, then on to Cripplegate and Aldersgate. From the latter place they went to Beech Lane, which was nearby; and here they killed a headborough or petty constable who tried to oppose them. With this second death on their hands, and with the hue and cry now widely raised against them, the rebels beat a swift retreat from the City, and retired northwards to the shelter of the woods in Ken Wood, Highgate. This locality was no doubt chosen because for long it had been a notorious haunt of Fifth Monarchy Men and their sympathizers.

Pepys, in his diary entry for 7 January 1661, recounted the sensational events of the night before (with some pardonable exaggerations due to the wild rumours circulating at the time): 'This morning, news was brought to me to my bed-side, that there had been a great stir in the City this night by the Fanatiques, who had been up and killed six or seven men, but all are fled. My Lord Mayor and the whole City had been in armes, above 40,000. . . .'

Pepys recounted how he and his wife visited the theatre on the evening of 7 January, and how, on their way home, they were 'in many places strictly examined, more than in the worst of times, there being great fears of the Fanatiques rising again;' but, Pepys added, 'for the present I do not hear that any of them are taken.'

Pepys was correct—at the time of the entry in his diary none of the rebels had been captured; and their bout of fanaticism had still to run its most violent course. The day after the tumult in the City the Government sent a detachment of horse and foot to Highgate in pursuit of the rebels, and as a result of this operation some thirty suspected Fifth Monarchy Men were rounded up and taken to the Gatehouse.[3] However, no trace could be found of Venner and his band.

These, still about fifty in number, soon made their presence known again in dramatic and bloody fashion. Early on Wednesday morning, 9 January, they left Highgate for the City, and were able to penetrate without trouble as far as Threadneedle Street. They then appeared before the Compter (or Counter) Prison on the north side of Poultry, and threatened to kill the warders if the prisoners were not released. By now the alarm had been raised, and though the men of one train-band were repulsed, reinforcements caused Venner and his men to retreat along Bishopsgate Street.

Here some of them appear to have been cut off from the main body, for they sought refuge in an ale-house called The Helmet. The men of the train-bands pursued them into the house, and after a sharp fight two Fifth Monarchy Men were killed and two more taken prisoner. The remainder of Venner's band suddenly re-emerged in Cheapside, and then turned into Wood Street, where they were again brought to a stand by two companies of train-bands.

Venner, with helmet on head and halberd in hand, the incarnation of Fifth Monarchy fanaticism, led his men in a furious fight with their adversaries, in which three of the latter were killed before the arrival of a detachment of lifeguards forced the Fifth Monarchy Men to give way once more. Most of the rebels, still fighting desperately, fled down Wood Street towards Cripplegate, firing as they ran from the train-bands pursuing them.

Two leading insurgents, Tufney and Cragg, had been killed, however; and Venner himself had been badly wounded in this clash, the fiercest of the day. The cohesion of the rebel band was, therefore, at last destroyed, and it broke up into small groups, each seeking its own escape route from the City through the maze of narrow streets and alleys.

Ten of the Fifth Monarchy Men, having arrived at the Postern

---

[3] A prison near the west end of Westminster Abbey. It was demolished in 1776.

at the east end of Fore Street, sought refuge in the nearby Blue Anchor Inn; and this was immediately besieged by the pursuing train-bands under Lieutenant-Colonel Cox.[4] The ten rebels climbed the stairs to the top room of the inn, and here they barricaded themselves in. Some members of the train-bands then entered an adjacent building, mounted to the attic, removed some tiles from the roof, and through the apertures thus made began to fire into the room where the Fifth Monarchy Men were holding out.

Meanwhile a file of musketeers had climbed the stairs of The Blue Anchor, and begun battering down the door of the room at the top. Harassed by the fire coming from the other building, the Fifth Monarchy Men found themselves in a hopeless position, and were unable to do anything to prevent the door being broken down. When the musketeers surged into the room they found six of the Fifth Monarchy Men dead on the floor, and another badly wounded. Of the remaining three one refused to surrender, and was immediately shot dead; and the remaining two were taken prisoner. As they were led away their captors asked them, in amazement at such determination, why they had not surrendered earlier, in view of the hopelessness of their position. In reply the prisoners declared that if they had shown the least sign of wishing to surrender, their comrades would have shot them on the spot.

Once again Pepys makes an illuminating entry in his diary for 9 January 1661, the day of the severe fighting:

Waked up in the morning about six o'clock, by people running up and down in Mr. Davis's house, talking that the Fanatiques were up in armes in the City. And so I rose and went forth; where in the street I found everybody in armes at the doors. So I returned and

---

[4] Pepys had a poor opinion of Cox. In his diary under 2 July 1666 he wrote:

Up betimes, and forced to go to my Lord Mayor's about the business of the pressed men. . . . Thence out of curiosity to Bridewell to see the pressed men. . . . Here I met with prating Col. Cox, one of the City colonells, heretofore a great presbyter; but to hear how the fellow did commend himself and the service he do the king; and, like an asse, at Paul's did take me out of my way on purpose to show me the gate (the little north gate) where he had two men shot close by him . . . and his own hair burnt by a bullet-shot in the insurrection of Venner, and himself escaped.

got my sword and pistol, which, however, I had no powder to charge; and went to the door, where I found Sir R. Ford [later, in 1671, Lord Mayor], and with him I walked up and down as far as the Exchange, and there I left him. In our way, the streets full of train-bands, and great stir. What mischief these rogues have done! And I think near a dozen had been killed this morning on both sides. The shops shut, and all things in trouble.

Pepys' figures with regard to the casualties on both sides were not accurate. Of the total of some fifty Fifth Monarchy Men involved in the insurrection, twenty-two had been killed and twenty, including the wounded Venner, taken prisoner. The few remaining who were captured subsequently were shot out of hand for refusing to divulge their names. The casualties on the other side were twenty-two killed, and a number wounded, the total of whom was not recorded.

It is astonishing that such a small body of insurgents convulsed the City and inflicted so many casualties on the much larger forces which were sent to deal with them. Pepys relates how the fanatical bravery of Venner and his followers led men to believe that they were far more numerous than in fact they were.

These Fanatiques [he wrote on 10 January 1661] that have routed all the train-bands that they met with, put the king's life-guards to the run, killed about twenty men, broke through the City-gates twice; and all this in the day time, when all the City was in armes; —are not in all above 31. Whereas we did believe them (because they were seen up and down in every place almost in the City, and had been in Highgate two or three days, and in several other places) to be at least 500. A thing that never was heard of, that so few men should dare and do so much mischief. Their word was 'The King Jesus, and their heads upon the gates!' Few of them would receive any quarter, but such as were taken by force and kept alive; expecting Jesus to come here and reign in the world presently. . . .

The bewilderment of contemporaries is understandable, for the events of the revolt were indeed chaotic; and even today, in the light of such evidence as has been handed down, it is not possible to piece together an entirely coherent account of what actually happened. Different accounts mention different places and give different figures, and it is only by comparing reports and accepting statements which seem to conform with the general pattern of events that a tolerably clear picture of the insurrection emerges.

On 16 January 1661 a pamphlet was published under the title:

The last farewel to the
Rebellious Sect
Called the Fifth
Monarchy–Men
on Wednesday January the Ninth,
Together with their Treacherous
Proceedings, Attempts, Combats and Skirmishes
at Woodstreet, Bishopsgate-Street, Leaden-
Hall, and several other places.
With the total Dispersing, Defeating and
utter Ruining of that Damnable and Seditious
Sect in General.

Though some of the facts and figures in this publication are almost certainly wrong, it does throw a little more light on what happened during the insurrection. The insurgents were said to have numbered nearly four hundred (a considerable over-estimate), and to have divided themselves into three parties. One of these (presumably that led by Venner) 'broke forth' from Bishopsgate at six o'clock in the morning, whilst another set out from near London Bridge. The members of this group, it was said,

were very excellent well-accoutred both for musquets, blunderbusses, barbines [a kind of barbed lance] and halberds, with buff-coats and helmets, both back and brest being thus completely armed; they marched in order, ranck and file down Canon-street, clearing the way as they went; they were led by Collonel Okey, who was seen by a Gentleman that knew him very well.[5]

This second group is said to have marched on from Cannon Street by way of Watling Street and Soper Lane (now Queen Street) into Cheapside, where presumably they must have joined Venner's party, and with them were subsequently driven back into Wood Street. After the dispersal of the Fifth Monarchists the men of this second group appear to have retreated by way of

---

[5] This is very doubtful. Okey, a regicide, had fled from England to Germany at the time of the Restoration.

Throgmorton Street and Cornhill. Near the Standard or conduit-pipe there they fought a brief but sharp engagement with a train-band and some foot soldiers, in which they lost five killed and one wounded. Three more were captured as the remaining rebels fled along Leadenhall Street and Gracechurch Street.

The third group of insurgents, whose activities were not specified, were said to have been defeated by the Lord Mayor and a troop of the City Horse, who also took some prisoners. All the time these operations were taking place the gates of the City were kept closed, all shops were shut, and the companies of trainbands were busy 'wheeling and traversing up and down the streets, and making search over all the City both for arms, armer, and traytors'.

By ten o'clock in the morning, with the dispersal and capture of the insurgents, the immediate danger was over; but ignorant of this James Duke of York, with General Monk (now Duke of Albemarle) at his right hand, and followed by seven hundred mounted lifeguards, and some five hundred noblemen, knights, and gentlemen, all mounted and armed, set off for the City to bring reinforcements to the Lord Mayor.

The latter met the new arrivals in Cheapside, at the head of the City Horse, and informed the Duke that the revolt had already been put down. The Duke thereupon thanked the Lord Mayor and all the brave citizens of London for their loyalty to their sovereign, and for so stoutly defending their laws and liberties; and having said this, he returned at the head of his cavalcade to Whitehall.

The insurrection had given the Government of Charles II a shock; and it dealt speedily and mercilessly with Venner and his surviving accomplices. On Thursday 17 January, Venner and nineteen others were brought to trial at Justice Hall in the Old Bailey, some still suffering so badly from the wounds which they had received that they were allowed to sit. All the prisoners were indicted for murder and high treason, and Venner was the first to be called to answer the charge.

On being asked whether he pleaded guilty or not guilty, he began 'an extravagant and bottomless discourse'[6] about the principles of the Fifth Monarchy, but finally, under pressure, pleaded

---

[6] Cobbett, *State Trials* (London 1810), Vol. VI, pp. 106–19.

Londons Glory,

OR,

The Riot and Ruine

Of the Fifth Monarchy Men, and
all their Adherents.

Being a true and perfect Relation of
their desperate and bloody Attempts and
Practises in the City of *London* on Monday, Tuesday, and Wednesday last,
Jan. the ninth, 1660.

Wherein by the *Loyal* and Valourous
behaviour of the *Citizens* in defence of
the Kings Majesty, their own Rights
and Priviledges ; they gave a total defeat to those bloody
TRAYTORS.

Together with a perfect *List* of the
names of all those that are taken Prisoners, and secured in *Newgate,* the
Powltry Counter and other
prisons.

Printed for C. D. 1661.

not guilty, a plea which was afterwards put forward by the other prisoners also. After evidence relating to the insurrection had been heard, the accused were asked what they had to say in their own defence. Venner, again called first, admitted that he had taken part in the revolt, but he denied that he had been the leader. When various witnesses were called to prove that he had been, Venner shifted his ground and declared that it was not he, but King Jesus, who had been the leader. Moreover, he added, he could not possibly be guilty of treason, because King Charles had not yet been crowned. He was told that as the King, in law, never dies, this plea was an irrelevance; and so he pursued it no further.

Of the other nineteen prisoners, fourteen admitted having taken part in the fighting, and four denied having borne arms, though they admitted that they had consorted with the other rebels. The remaining prisoner, John Wells, stated that Venner had made him bear arms on pain of having his throat cut if he disobeyed; but he declared that at the first opportunity he had flung down his sword and pistol, and had run away.

Wells and three others (including two who had declared themselves innocent of bearing arms) were acquitted by the jury; but the sixteen other prisoners and Venner were found guilty, and sentenced to death for high treason. However the full barbaric punishment for that crime, hanging, drawing and quartering, was, by exercise of the royal clemency, carried out on only two of the condemned men, Venner himself and Roger Hodgkin, a button-seller, who was one of Venner's chief lieutenants. These two were put to death in the manner prescribed by law, outside their meeting-place in Swan Alley, Coleman Street.

On Saturday 19 January, the two Fifth Monarchy Men, still suffering from the wounds they had received, were drawn on a sledge guarded by two companies of the City train-bands from Newgate Prison, along Cheapside to the place of execution in Coleman Street. The ubiquitous Pepys, as he noted in his diary on that date, saw the unhappy wretches as they went on their last journey: 'January 19, To the Comptroller's, and with him by coach to Whitehall; in our way meeting Venner and Pritchard[7] upon a sledge, who with two more Fifth Monarchy

---

[7] Pepys appears to have confused Pritchard with Hodgkin.

Men were hanged today, and the two first drawn and quartered.'

Before sentence was carried out on him Venner was allowed to speak; but he was subdued, and, true to the last to his Fifth Monarchy principles, merely warned the crowd that the time was at hand 'when other judgement would be'. Hodgkin, on the other hand, on seeing Venner despatched, worked himself up into a frenzy, and from the scaffold cried in a loud voice to heaven for vengeance on the King, the judges, and the City of London. The Sheriff commanded him to stop; but Hodgkin, in a paroxysm of demented fury, still went on. The hangman was therefore hurriedly summoned from his station nearby, where he was busy hacking Venner's body into quarters, and he at once put an end to Hodgkin's ravings.

The quarters of the two Fifth Monarchy Men were placed upon the City gates, which had already received the quartered bodies of the lately executed regicides; but the two heads, according to custom, were put on the top of poles at the south end of London Bridge. Subsequently the other condemned men were executed, a batch of nine being hanged on 21 January at different places in the City—Wood Street, Beech Lane, Bishopsgate, Aldersgate, the Royal Exchange, and the west end of St. Paul's —where the fighting had been fiercest during the revolt.

In addition to executing those persons found guilty of having taken part in the insurrection, the Government took no chance with other prominent Fifth Monarchy Men whom it suspected, but against whom no definite evidence of plotting against the regime could be brought. Major-General Overton, arrested in December 1660 and sent to the Tower of London, was kept in custody, except for a short period in 1663, until his death in 1668. Quartermaster-General Courtney, arrested in January 1661, was kept in the Gatehouse till 19 June; but then released on condition that he left the country within fifteen days and did not return.

The Government's severity against those involved in the plot, also against those whom it suspected of complicity, was designed to deter those of the brethren who remained at large from seeking to emulate Venner and his comrades. Nevertheless, for many years to come rumours and reports of further plans for revolt continued to come in and alarm the authorities. For much longer still, down to the present day, the millenarian doctrines of the Fifth Monarchy Men survived; and their propagation by small groups of devoted adherents enlivened the English religious scene from time to time with episodes in which the tragic was mingled with the grotesque.

9

FAITH WITHOUT WORKS

DESPITE the executions of January 1661 the Fifth Monarchy Men, undaunted, continued to hold meetings and propagate the faith. The Quakers had quite unjustifiably come under suspicion at the time of Venner's revolt in January 1661; and George Fox, annoyed when he heard that the Fifth Monarchy Men, persisting in their beliefs, were now proclaiming that Christ would come to inaugurate the millennium in 1666, was moved, so he related in his journal, 'to give forth a paper to them'. They thought, he said, that they were to 'kill the whore'; but, he affirmed, the whore was not outside them, but alive within them.[1]

Undeterred by the strictures of Fox and other opponents, the Fifth Monarchy Men continued their clandestine activities. On 9 February information came to the authorities that some sixteen members of the sect were gathering together two or three times a week at the Maiden Head Tavern in Piccadilly; and other groups revived also as the saints slowly regathered their strength. On 1 April an informer reported to the Government that the Fifth Monarchy Men were exhorting one another in their congregations to suffer rather than pollute their consciences; and on 18 April the Fifth Monarchists were once again preaching sedition at one of their notorious haunts, Christ Church, Newgate. Here in traditional style they demanded that all shedders of 'righteous blood' should be called strictly to account.

Earlier in the month a plot had been hatched by some Fifth Monarchy Men to stage an armed revolt on Monday 15 April, when the King would be at Windsor. The news of this leaked out to the authorities however, and various houses were searched and a number of suspects arrested, and the plot, such as it was, collapsed.[2]

---

[1] Fox, *Journal* (edited N. Penney, Cambridge 1911), Vol. II, p. 12.

[2] *The Traytors Unvailed* (18 April 1661).

In August 1661 there were further reports of Fifth Monarchist activity. About thirty of them held a meeting at Norton Folgate, a place near Bishopsgate Green, and were said to be 'laying plots and preparing for trouble'.[3] Groups were meeting in September as boldly as they had done before Venner's rising, and members of the sect declared that their hopes were higher than ever before, and that they were convinced that King Charles II and his bishops were heading fast to their own destruction. One Belchar, who had been a leading preacher at the meeting-place in Swan Alley under Venner, but had fallen out with him, was reported to be busy in the Limehouse district, preaching to the people and trying to seduce them from their allegiance to the King.[4]

In November members of the sect were said to be 'strongly at work' in places as far apart as Yorkshire, Durham, East Anglia, and Devonshire; and some leading exponents of the faith, including Mr. Palmer, Mr. Elmes, Mr. Belchar, and Mr. Feake, were busy travelling from county to county trying to 'blow the flames of rebellion'. In London the centre of activities was in Limehouse, at the house of a rich brewer named Andrews, where frequent meetings were held. William Medley was the 'scribe, accountant and keeper of the papers' of this group, thus fulfilling a function which he had had once before, at the time of Venner's first revolt in 1657. Another member of the sect who had been involved in the 1657 plot, a woman named Harding, was also prominent at the meetings in Andrews' house, and was thought sufficiently trustworthy for important documents to be committed to her care.[5]

Whenever it was possible the Government took action against the sectaries. Thus on 22 November 1661 a Fifth Monarchist preacher named John James was sentenced to death for high treason because of his preaching activities at a meeting-place in Bulstake Alley, Whitechapel. James, a coalman, had been one of Venner's associates, but had not taken part in the insurrection of January 1661. He continued afterwards to address meetings of Fifth Monarchy Men, and was ultimately betrayed to the authorities by his neighbours.

---

[3] *Calendar of State Papers Domestic*, 27 August 1661.
[4] Ibid., 26 September 1661.   [5] Ibid., 2 November 1661.

James was executed at Tyburn on 26 November, and some idea of the fanaticism of his fellow-Fifth Monarchy Men can be gained from a contemporary account of what happened. On the way to Tyburn, it was said, 'divers of his followers took their leave of him, shewing many expressions and demonstrations of kindness towards him, throwing themselves, as he passed, into the sledge where he was drawn, and there embracing him. . . .'[6]

To discourage these and any other enthusiasts, James' head was impaled upon a pole which was erected in the centre of Bulstake Alley, near to the meeting-place where he had been wont to preach. This grim warning had little effect, for in the early part of June 1662 Fifth Monarchy Men were holding meetings in the parish of St. Olave's, Southwark, and an order had to be sent to the Justices of the Peace to take action against them. Again, on 12 June there was a scare that the Fifth Monarchists and Baptists might combine and attempt an insurrection; and the Lord Mayor of London and the Duke of Albemarle were warned of this possibility by the Secretary of State, Sir Edward Nicholas. The rumours, however, proved false.

Perhaps because of the unsettled conditions and spate of alarmist rumours the Government decided that a show of firmness and force would be salutary. At all events, in June 1662 the decision was taken to bring Sir Henry Vane, a noted friend of the Fifth Monarchists, back to London from his imprisonment in the Scilly Isles, and to put him on trial for high treason. Vane had played a prominent part in affairs after the death of Oliver Cromwell, but had become generally disliked and distrusted by both Parliament and Army because of his political manoeuvres, which, it was rumoured, had as their aim the establishment of a republican theocracy akin to the conception of the Fifth Monarchy Men.

Though Vane had taken no part in the trial of King Charles I, his republican principles and record were enough to damn him when the Restoration took place; and he was excluded, like the regicides, from the Act of Indemnity of August 1660 which extended a general clemency to those who had opposed the King. Vane had not been brought to trial, however, but had been imprisoned, first in the Tower of London, then in the Scilly Isles.

---

[6] Pagitt, *Heresiography* (London 1662), p. 295.

When put on trial Vane pleaded not guilty, and advanced the same argument in his defence that Major-General Harrison had used, namely that all his actions had been based on the authority of Parliament, and that their legitimacy could not be called in question by any lower court. Like Harrison's, his pleas were brushed aside, and he was found guilty and sentenced to death. The execution took place on Tower Hill on 14 June 1662, and Vane, dressed elegantly for the occasion in a black suit with a scarlet waistcoat, so impressed the spectators by his brave demeanour that orders were given to the troops standing by to sound their trumpets and to beat their drums, so that his last words to the crowd should be unheard. Pepys witnessed the execution, and wrote an account of it in his diary:

June 14. About 11 o'clock, having a room got ready for us, we all went out to the Tower-hill; and there, over against the scaffold, made on purpose this day, saw Sir Henry Vane brought. A very great press of people. He made a long speech, many times interrupted by the Sheriffe, and others there; and they would have taken his paper out of his hand, but he would not let it go. But they caused all the books of those that writ after him [i.e. making notes of his speech] to be given to the Sheriffe; and the trumpets were brought under the scaffold that he might not be heard. Then he prayed, and so fitted himself, and received the blow; but the scaffold was so crowded that we could not see it done ... He had a blister or issue upon his neck, which he desired them not to hurt; he changed not his colour or his speech to the last, but died justifying himself and the cause he had stood for.... So [Pepys nonchalantly concluded] to the office a little, and to the Trinity-house, and there all of us to dinner.

Vane had given another very singular proof of his composure during the night before his execution. His wife had been admitted to his cell to take leave of him; and he deliberately made known the next morning, just before he was drawn on the sledge to the place of execution, that he had had intercourse with her. This he revealed, he said, lest any aspersions should be cast on her afterwards if she became pregnant.[7]

Vane's last words before he died clearly indicated his Fifth

---

[7] *Bishop Burnet's History of His Own Time* (edited M. J. Routh, Oxford 1823), Vol. I, p. 279.

Monarchy sympathies. 'The coming of Christ', he declared, 'in order to a sudden and speedy revival of his cause, and spreading his kingdom over the face of the whole earth, is most clear to the eye of my faith, even that faith in which I die!'[8]

Contemporaries differed in their opinion of him; but perhaps Clarendon summed him up best when he described him as:

A man of extraordinary parts, a pleasant wit, a great understanding, which pierced into and discerned the purposes of other men with wonderful sagacity, whilst he had himself *vultum clausum* [literally 'a closed face'] that no man could make a guess of what he intended. He was of a temper not to be moved, and of rare dissimulation.[9]

In Sir Henry Vane the Fifth Monarchy Men had lost a once influential friend and ally; but despite the warning which his execution was intended to convey, the members of the sect continued their subversive activities, and many arrests were made. For example, on 22 June 1662, of 117 prisoners in the Surrey county gaol, nearly all were Fifth Monarchy Men. The sect was flourishing in other, more distant counties too, and reports of Fifth Monarchist meetings came from Hatfield, the Isle of Axholme, Doncaster, and Durham. From the latter place an informant reported in September 1663 that members of the sect were 'in the same mind that they were in Venner's business', and that they were making preparations 'to finish the Lord's work, as they call it'.[10]

Despite such alarmist rumours, however, the activities of the Fifth Monarchy Men were so scattered and circumscribed that the Duke of Albemarle, writing from London to the Earl of Winchilsea on 28 December 1663, could say: 'All things here are well. Now and then there are some little designs amongst the Anabaptists and Fifth Monarchy Men, which are a people will never be quiett, butt their designes are so weake and inconsiderable that I am confident they will nott bee dangerous to his Majesty and the Kingdome.'[11]

---

[8] Cobbett, *State Trials*, Vol. VI, p. 198.

[9] *History of the Rebellion and Civil Wars in England* (Oxford 1888), Vol. III, p. 216.

[10] *Calendar of State Papers Domestic*, 22 September 1663.

[11] *Historical MSS. Commission*, MSS of A. G. Finch, Vol. I, p. 299.

In the latter part of 1663 the Fifth Monarchists were active in Dorking and neighbourhood. The reason for this was that Christopher Feake, who had settled at Chipstead, some seven miles away, had begun once again to preach surreptitiously against the Government. News of his renewed activities came to the notice of the local authorities, and on 4 January 1664 the two deputy Lord Lieutenants of Surrey informed the Secretary of State, Sir Edward Brett, that Feake was a dangerous man. Many libellous publications, they said, were brought every week from London to Feake's home, and he would undoubtedly seduce many people of Dorking and neighbourhood from their lawful allegiance, unless he was restrained.

As a result of this information a warrant was issued for Feake's arrest on a charge of seditious practices. On 5 January, when soldiers came to his house to carry out the warrant, they found the doors locked and bolted against them, and had to break them down by force before Feake would surrender. As he was led away he declared angrily that he did not look with favour on the Government, and was ready to suffer for his opinions like Shadrach, Meshech, and Abednego.[12]

He lost his equanimity, however, when he heard that he was to be taken to London. He had become very unpopular there since Venner's revolt, for he was commonly regarded as one of the chief instigators of it. Threats had been made against his life, and it was no doubt because he wished to escape his enemies that he had moved to the rural seclusion of Surrey. His fears grew less when he heard that he would have an escort of soldiers on the journey; and during a long examination to which he was subjected before being taken away he showed himself much less defiant than hitherto.

He declared that he had not taken part in any church activities for the past two or three years, nor had he attended any unlawful assemblies. Only the members of his own family, he said, had been present at the services which he had held. Feake then asserted that he had never received from London books or

---

[12] The names given by Nebuchadnezzar's chief eunuch to Daniel's three companions in captivity (Daniel i. 7), who were cast into a fiery furnace because they would not worship the golden image which Nebuchadnezzar had set up (Daniel iii).

pamphlets containing seditious matter; and he maintained that he had taken the oath of allegiance to King Charles II.

His rather abject defence availed him little, however; for he appears to have been kept in custody until 25 July 1664. On that date he was released, after promising that he would live peaceably in the future, abstain from anti-government activities, and present himself whenever summoned by the Government. He must have kept his undertaking, for after 1664 there is no further mention of him. It must be presumed, therefore, that even if he did not forswear his Fifth Monarchy beliefs, he renounced the propagation of them. This must be accounted a tame and ignominious withdrawal by one who had played a leading part during a decade in rousing the Fifth Monarchy rank and file, and who had proudly proclaimed, many and many a time, that he was ready to die for the cause.

The end for John Rogers, Feake's old fellow-prisoner of the Lord and fellow-adept in rabble-rousing, was equally inglorious. Rogers had welcomed the recall of the Rump in May 1659, and he had supported it in its disputes with the Army. In July 1659 the Council of State had rewarded him by appointing him as preacher of the Gospel in Galloway, Ireland; but Rogers decided that he would prefer to remain in England, and on 19 September he was released from the undertaking which he had previously given that he would take up the post. On 13 October, at the request of a number of citizens of Shrewsbury, he was appointed public preacher in that town; but for some reason unknown he did not go to Shrewsbury but went, after all, to Ireland. There he fell foul of the authorities and was for a time imprisoned in Dublin, until 27 January 1660, when the Council of State, at the request of Mrs. Rogers, instructed the Commissioners in Ireland to release him.

When he perceived that the return of Charles II was inevitable, Rogers fled to the Netherlands. There he resumed medical studies which he had followed for a short time as a young man, and in October 1662 he was granted the degree of M.D. by the University of Utrecht. Some time after this he was allowed to return to England, no doubt on condition that he took no further part in Fifth Monarchist activities, for, in fact, there is no more mention of his name in connexion with the sect.

Henceforth he gained a living practising as a doctor in

Bermondsey, and as late as 1665 he was advertising 'alexiterial and antipestilential medicine, an admirable and experimented preservative from the plague'. This, however, was the last to be heard of him; so it may well be that despite the properties of his antipestilential medicine, he was one of the many people in London who fell victims in 1665 to the Great Plague.

In March 1665 there were reports of yet another Fifth Monarchy plot against the Government, in which the King and the Duke of Albemarle were to be assassinated, and Whitehall taken by storm—but once again nothing came of this, the sober members preferring to bide their time. The leading spirit among the London Fifth Monarchists at this time was a man named Helmes, who seems to have taken the place of Feake as agitator in chief; but dissensions within the sect about the policy to be adopted, which continued into 1666, weakened it. The fact that no advantage was taken of the confusion and dismay evoked by the Great Fire of London, a catastrophe occurring most significantly in the year which contained 666, the number of the Beast, reflects the increasing weakness and disarray of the Fifth Monarchy Men. This seems to have been due partly to a general feeling of disillusion, partly to the gradual ascendancy within the movement of the non-militant elements.

In March 1668, for example, an informant reported to the Government that at a meeting in Blue Anchor Alley, Old Street, a leading Herefordshire Fifth Monarchy Man, a scholar, had asserted that the main task was to understand the language of Christ, their Lord and King, and to be ready to act when he called—but not before. Moreover, the speaker added, the only sensible policy was to act with the greatest prudence, at all times avoiding danger.

The informant stated that Vavasor Powell was due to speak at the meeting in Blue Anchor Alley on the following Sunday. This must have been during one of Powell's brief periods of freedom from imprisonment. After the Restoration he continued his wanderings in Wales, preaching Baptist and Fifth Monarchy doctrines, and obstinately refusing to take the oaths of allegiance and supremacy. For his contumacy he was imprisoned for lengthy periods; and still remaining quite unregenerate during his latest spell of freedom in 1668, was sent to the Fleet Prison, where he died in 1670.

With Powell's disappearance from the scene the last vestiges of fire in the Fifth Monarchy movement died out, and references to the sect's activities became fewer and fewer. In June 1671 John Bellchar, a bricklayer whom the Government's informants described as a Fifth Monarchist and 'a most notorious knave from Oxfordshire'[13] was preaching at an unlawful assembly in Bell Lane, Spitalfields. As a result of the evidence brought against him, Bellchar and three others, including Arthur Squib, a Fifth Monarchy Man of long standing, were committed to the Tower of London on the ground that they were dangerous persons. At the same time twenty-seven members of the congregation were sent to Newgate, and on 18 July were required to take the oath of allegiance to Charles II. Since they all refused, they were kept in custody, and all their possessions were declared forfeited.

Despite the decline of the sect, fear of the Fifth Monarchy Men lingered on, and was revived as a result of the confusion engendered by the alleged Popish Plot in 1678. Even King Charles II, who was sceptical about the information which Titus Oates produced to substantiate his allegations about the Popish Plot, believed that Fifth Monarchy Men might still be actively preparing for an insurrection. The King was even disposed to believe that it was these, the Fifth Monarchy Men, and not the alleged Catholic plotters, who were rumoured from all parts of the kingdom 'to be riding up and down in small parties in the night'.[14]

There are isolated references to members of the sect in the reign of James II, but it is clear that by then they were no longer regarded as a potentially dangerous force. In fact, the fire had long since completely gone out of Fifth Monarchism; and all that was left was the peaceful propagation of the millenarian faith.

The persistence of the belief in the imminence of Christ's return to earth to found his kingdom was reflected in the strange events which took place at Water Stratford in Buckinghamshire in 1694. John Mason, a graduate of Cambridge University, and from 1674 rector of Water Stratford, became more and more convinced not only that Christ would soon return to establish his personal reign on earth, but that he would choose to come to

---

[13] *Calendar of State Papers Domestic*, 1 July 1671.
[14] *Historical MSS Commission*, Ormonde MSS., New Series, Vol. IV, p. 486.

Water Stratford to do it. Mason attracted a small band of followers, and these decided to settle in Water Stratford to await the return of Christ. They encamped on a small plot which was called 'The Holy Ground', and lived there in communal fashion when not engaged in services which were held day and night in the rectory, to the accompaniment of singing and dancing.

Mason told his followers that on Easter Monday, 16 April 1694, he had been vouchsafed a vision of Christ; and he assured his followers that though the Saviour had not yet appeared in person at Water Stratford, he had already begun his reign on earth. In conformity with this belief Mason henceforth omitted the opening words of the Lord's Prayer, 'Our Father, which art in Heaven . . .' in the services which he conducted.

The faithful band of followers suffered a severe shock in May 1694, for Mason died of an inflammation of the throat, and was buried in his parish churchyard. His supporters, however, stubbornly refused to believe that their prophet could have succumbed to earthly ills; and the parson who had succeeded Mason judged it wise to have the latter's body exhumed, so that it could be shown beyond a doubt that he was dead. Even then some of the more obstinate members of Mason's flock refused to depart from the 'Holy Ground', and eventually they had to be removed by force. Despite this, meetings of the faithful continued to be held in a house in Water Stratford for a further sixteen years; and a belief in Mason's resurrection persisted even longer, till death picked off one by one the remaining members.

Millenarian enthusiasm had always flourished when men thought and cared deeply about religion, and when political convulsions tempted them to deduce that the time of the end was approaching. For these reasons Fifth Monarchism was essentially a creed of the seventeenth century. In the eighteenth century, an age of reason and growing scepticism, and of internal stability, the ethos was lacking, and millenarianism declined into insignificance. At the end of the century, however, the French Revolution and the rise of Napoleon inaugurated another period of political conflict and uncertainty; and there was a corresponding revival of interest in millenarian ideas, reflected in the careers of Richard Brothers, Joanna Southcott, and John Wroe.

In the late nineteenth century the tradition was carried on by the ex-private of the Bedfordshire Regiment who called himself

James Jershom Jezreel; and even in (or perhaps because of) the present materialistic age latter-day disciples of Jezreel, and other exponents of millenarian views, can still be heard discoursing at Speakers' Corner by Marble Arch. Here, to the unregenerate, they propound theses which would undoubtedly have won the assent of Feake, Rogers, Harrison, and other eminent spiritual brethren of an earlier and more godly generation.

10

A STIFF-NECKED PEOPLE

It is quite impossible to estimate, even approximately, the numbers and strength of the Fifth Monarchy movement in the seventeenth century. One reason for this is that the name 'Fifth Monarchy Man' tended to be given indiscriminately to persons of a wide range of opinions and beliefs, from peaceful dreamers to bellicose fanatics, whose only common ground was a belief in the approach of the millennium. For example, there were those, and they were many, who believed that the millennium would certainly be inaugurated by Christ in person, but who did not necessarily believe that his return was imminent, nor that the biblical prophecies concerning the beasts and the horns should be related to contemporary kingdoms.

People of this sort, who were certainly millenarians, but kept an open mind with regard to the niceties of the faith as expounded by preachers such as John Rogers and Christopher Feake, are perhaps better described as Fifth Monarchist sympathizers or 'part Fifth Monarchy Men'. Major-General Goffe, for example, has been described as 'three-quarters a Fifth Monarchy Man',[1] and many Baptists and Army men of republican principles can be included in the same category, though the degree of their affinity depended on their individual temperament. Thus the republican Sir Henry Vane, though he never in his writings specifically subscribed to the full Fifth Monarchy doctrines, was undoubtedly a millenarian like Goffe, and was, moreover, on close and friendly terms with persons like John Rogers who were leading exponents of the Fifth Monarchy faith.

Even within the ranks of the Fifth Monarchists proper there were dissensions which led to divisions. A majority, whilst fully accepting the interpretation of the prophetic books of the Bible

---

[1] C. H. Firth, *Clarke Papers* (London 1891–1901), Vol. I, Preface, lxxiii–lxxiv.

which identified the Little Horn with Charles I or Cromwell, and therefore accepting, too, that the time of Christ's coming was near, yet refused to take any positive forceful action to hasten it. Henry Archer was one of the writers who expressed the views of these pacific brethren. In his *Personall Reign of Christ upon Earth* (1642), after affirming his belief that Christ would soon 'visibly possesse a monarchical State and Kingdom in this world', he asked: 'What use should we make of all this doctrine about Christ's Kingdome?' In reply, however, he came to the rather inglorious conclusion that the saints could only look for and long for the Kingdom, since they could not in any way hasten its coming.

William Aspinwall, too, went to great pains to demonstrate that the Fifth Monarchy Men were not the ogres they were commonly supposed to be. On the contrary, Aspinwall declared, they were 'the best and truest friends unto Government, and count it their duty to be faithful unto their trust, be the rulers what they may'.

Aspinwall, indeed, went so far as to assert that 'Saints may officiate under wicked and prophane princes and rulers', in reply to the question: 'Whether may not Christians, that wait for this Kingdom of Christ, submit unto Civil Powers under the Fourth Monarchy, and also act under them?'[2]

This accommodating doctrine was not to the liking of other Fifth Monarchy Men, who were impatient to end the Fourth Monarchy by force. They were a minority, however, chiefly concentrated in London, and on the two occasions when they tried by force to hasten the coming of Christ, the more prudent brethren stood aside. The revolts failed, and the Fifth Monarchy movement suffered accordingly.

There were other dissensions within the sect with regard to what might be called doctrinal matters. One fruitful cause of controversy was the exact identification of the Little Horn, that baleful manifestation of Antichrist, the end of whose dominion was to usher in the rule of the saints. For some Fifth Monarchy thinkers the Papacy remained forever identified with the Little Horn; others fixed on Charles I; and others again, feeling that

---

[2] *The Legislative Power is Christ's Peculiar Prerogative* (1656), pp. 36–37.

events had rendered that particular identification invalid, plumped for Oliver Cromwell. The controversy, though spirited, was usually carried on in polite fashion by the brethren. Thus in August 1654 John More published a pamphlet entitled: 'The Second Sounding of the Little Horn, or A further prosecution of the great Mystery of the Two Little Horns'.

More referred to Aspinwall's *Explication and Application of the Seventh Chapter of Daniel*, in which Charles I had been proved to be the Little Horn. Disclaiming any intention of being offensive to Aspinwall, and emphasizing that he, More, was certainly no partisan of Charles I, he went on to prove that the latter could not possibly be the Little Horn; and he revealed triumphantly that that unenviable distinction had been reserved by fate for 'Oliver, Lord Protector so-called'.

Aspinwall's theory evoked another refutation by Rhys Evans, who also believed in the imminence of the Fifth Monarchy, but whose interpretation of the portents was unorthodox and fantastic in the extreme. Evans, born in Merionethshire in 1607, appeared in London in 1629 and worked for a time as a tailor. He became a prey to religious mania, however, and claimed that he saw visions which enabled him to prophesy the future. In accordance with this new role he dropped the prosaic name Rhys, and called himself henceforth Arise Evans.

What particularly aroused his opposition to Aspinwall was the identification of Charles I with the Little Horn, for Evans was a passionate supporter of the late King and Archbishop Laud. In refutation of Aspinwall's *Brief Description of the Fifth Monarchy* he published on 10 December 1655 a counterblast entitled: 'A Refutation of a Pamphlet lately published by one Aspinwall: called A Brief Discription of the Fifth Monarchy.'

In this Evans first of all castigated Feake, Simpson, and the other orthodox Fifth Monarchists, 'the murmuring people', he said, 'that meet every Munday in Blackfriers Church'. Those exponents of the faith, he declared, were 'not for the interest of Jesus Christ, as they falsely affirm, but are for the interest of the Devil!' He agreed with Aspinwall that the Fifth Monarchy would shortly begin, but he asserted that it would be established in the person of Charles II, and that the event would take place in 1667. The calculations by which he arrived at that date were ludicrous, even by Fifth Monarchy standards. The late Archbishop

Laud, he said, was called VVILLIaM LaVD. No account was to
be taken of the little letter 'a' in the name; but the other letters,
which were Roman numerals, added together came to 1667,
since M was 1000, DLL was 600, LVV was 60, and VII was 7.

It is gratifying to record that Evans' devotion to the Stuarts
was ultimately rewarded, though in a singular way. He lived to
see the Restoration, and to be touched by Charles II for scrofula,
called the 'King's Evil' because, so it was believed, it could be
cured by the royal touch. John Aubrey, a contemporary, wrote:
'Arise Evans had a fungous nose, and said it was revealed to him
that the King's hand would cure him; and at the first coming of
King Charles II into St. James' Park he kissed the King's hand,
and rubbed his nose with it; which disturbed the King, but cured
him.'[3]

The chronological calculations in which Arise Evans showed
such originality were also a fruitful cause of controversy among
the orthodox Fifth Monarchy Men, who devoted much time and
labour to the task of ascertaining for the benefit of the faithful the
time of the end. Elaborate computations were always involved,
and a knowledge of both ancient history and mathematics was
necessary to comprehend fully the arguments advanced in
favour of the different theories.

Dr. John Pell, English Ambassador to the Swiss Cantons,
writing to the Secretary of State, John Thurloe, on 17 March
1655 referred to some of the conflicting Fifth Monarchist calculations of the time of the end.

Some [he wrote] that have heard that the end of Paganism is placed
in the year 395, and that then there was not one heathen temple
left standing in the Roman Empire, will easily be induced to believe that the famous number, 1260,[4] ought to be added to it; and
then this year, 1655, must needs be pointed out for an apocalyp-
tical epocha. Others pitch upon the year 1656, because, having
summed up the lives of the patriarchs in the fifth chapter of
Genesis, they find 1656 years from the Creation to the Flood, and
thence infer that the coming of Christ will be the next year, because
it must be as in the days of Noah.

---

[3] Aubrey, *Miscellanies* (4th edition, London 1857), p. 128.
[4] 'And the woman fled into the wilderness, where she hath a
place prepared of God, that they should feed her there a thousand
two hundred and threescore days' (Revelation xii. 6).

Dr. Pell went on to relate that other theorists added twice the number of the Beast, which was 666 (Revelation xiii. 18), and then added the total, 1332, to the year of the Council of Nice in A.D. 325, and thus arrived at the year 1657 as the time of the end. Others, again, with the number of the Beast in mind, thought that the year 1666 must infallibly be the appointed time.[5]

Though the age was one when credulity flourished, especially in relation to religion, the painstaking efforts of the Fifth Monarchy Men to forecast the beginning of the millennium met with a good deal of scepticism, and were freely held up to ridicule. 'In their lectures and conventicles', a contemporary writer sarcastically remarked, 'you might have heard such raptures that you would have thought it were a reading on Astrology.... Months, weeks, daies, and half-times and such-like chronology alwaies past away their mad hours of meeting.'[6]

On the other hand, in an age when the Bible was interpreted literally, there were not wanting many educated and intelligent men who, whilst not necessarily subscribing to any particular Fifth Monarchist theory about the time of the end, nevertheless believed that a careful search of the Bible would enable this to be ascertained. Even such geniuses as Napier of Merchiston and Sir Isaac Newton devoted themselves to prolonged studies of the chronology of the prophetic books of the Bible in order to arrive at a satisfactory solution of the mysteries contained in them.

John Napier of Merchiston, the inventor of logarithms, published in 1593 his *Plaine Discovery of the Whole Revelation of St. John.* This quickly went through several editions in the first half of the seventeenth century in England, and was translated into several European languages. Napier went to infinite trouble to explain in precise mathematical terms such prophetic phrases as 'a time, and times, and half a time' (Revelation xii. 14), in order to find out when the Day of Judgement would occur; and his conclusions led him to forecast that it would probably fall between the years 1688 and 1700.

For Napier of Merchiston the interpretation of the prophetic books had a twofold interest and fascination: it was a religious study, but at the same time an intricate mathematical problem

---

[5] Vaughan, *The Protectorate of Oliver Cromwell* (London 1838), Vol. I, pp. 155–7.

[6] Pagitt, *Heresiography* (1662), p. 282.

to be solved. The same motives impelled an even greater man, Sir Isaac Newton, to spend much of his time on the elucidation of the books of Daniel and Revelation; and his conclusions were published posthumously in 1733 under the title: *Observations upon the Prophecies of Daniel and the Apocalypse of St. John.*

Newton declared that to reject Daniel's prophecies was to reject the Christian religion; and he proceeded to interpret Daniel's vision with a wealth of detailed chronological data. Even when he came to the baffling problem of the identification of the Little Horn Newton had no doubts, and unhesitatingly, like a good Protestant, cast the Papacy for this unpopular role. In his observations on the Apocalypse of St. John he revealed that he believed the time of the end was approaching.

It was [he wrote] a part of the prophecy [Revelation] that it should not be understood before the last age of the world; and therefore it makes for the credit of the prophecy that it is not yet understood. But if the last age, the age of opening these things, be now approaching, as by the great successes of late interpreters it seems to be, we have more encouragement than ever to look into these things. (pp. 250–1.)

Lesser men than Newton had likewise been encouraged to 'look into these things'; and although the extravagant deductions and calculations of the Fifth Monarchy Men must be regarded as pathetically naïve, at least, seen in the perspective of Napier and Newton, the devotion and effort that went into the elaboration of their fantastic theories become more understandable.

The political and economic thinking of the Fifth Monarchy Men, if not quite as ingenuous as their millenarian computations, was, in comparison with the ideas put forward by other political theorists of the age, shallow and limited in range. The sect produced no thinker or writer of the calibre of Harrington or Hobbes; and the reason for this is not far to seek. Believing as they did in the pre-ordained right of the elect, that is, the company of saints, to rule the Kingdom under King Jesus, in accordance with divine laws, they considered any elaborate exposition of the theory of government as unnecessary.

Similarly, when on occasion they listed particular reforms which they said ought to be carried out (as Rogers, for example, did in *Sagrir*), these were not objectively set down as part of a comprehensive, carefully thought out system introducing a new political and social order, but were isolated reforms arbitrarily chosen—often because the existing practices which they were designed to change bore heavily on the saints.

These criticisms are applicable to the two manifestos, *A Standard Set Up* (1657) and *A Door of Hope* (1660), which outlined the Fifth Monarchy programme. The authors of *A Standard Set Up* said that they would 'state, under some generall heads, the cause we plead for and the work we desire to prosecute'; and the proposals set forth in that document are also, in general, reproduced in the later *A Door of Hope*.

The country was to be ruled by a Sanhedrim or Supreme Council, whose members, according to *A Standard Set Up*, would be 'men of choicest light and spirit, indued with judgment, righteousnesse, wisdom, knowledge, understanding, able men, men of truth, and of known integrity, fearing God, haters of covetousnesse, being filled with the fruits of righteousnesse, full of mercy and good works, without partiality, and without hypocrisie'.

These paragons were to be chosen 'according to the principle of right and freedom'; and a little elucidation was given later of this somewhat vague statement. The Supreme Council was to be representative 'of the whole body of the Saints', and was to be elected for a period of a year at a time by the 'Lord's Freemen', who were defined as 'those that have a right with Christ in and according to the new covenant'.

Though the provision for re-election of the Supreme Council at the end of a twelve-month period anticipated the proposal of the Chartists in the early nineteenth century that there should be annual parliaments, in general the political proposals of the Fifth Monarchists must be viewed with reserve. If words had any meaning at all, the Supreme Council would have been chosen only from the saints, and by the saints; and it would therefore have been a body quite unrepresentative of the people as a whole.

The implications of the Fifth Monarchist political proposals become even more questionable in the light of the principles by which, it was suggested, the Supreme Council should govern. *A Standard Set Up* declared that the Scriptures were the revealed will of Christ, the supreme lawgiver, and were to be taken, therefore, as the guide in the government of the country. *A Door of*

Hope echoed this, declaring that Christ's laws and statutes contained in the Holy Scriptures were to be 'the law by which these nations shall be governed and judged'.

Though *A Standard Set Up* asserted that 'the oppressed and almost devoured people' would be refreshed and revived by an administration conducted according to laws based on the Scriptures, large questions were left unanswered. For example, *A Door of Hope* categorized 'the greatest sins', and stated that they were 'swearing, drunkenness, sabbath-breaking, whoredome, pride, lasciviousness, stage-plays, blasphemy, popery, superstition, idolatry'. The inference was unmistakable. Under a regime based on divine laws as revealed in the Scriptures and interpreted by the saints, such sins would be severely punished. Though (again to quote from *A Door of Hope*) the great desire of the Fifth Monarchists was 'to take off all yoaks and oppressions both of a civil and spiritual nature from the necks of the poor people', who can doubt that new yokes and oppressions would have been introduced in their place?

When the new regime had been established, the authors of *A Door of Hope* confidently predicted, its subjects would be 'the happiest people in the world, having the best laws and the best governors'. Judged by the austere standards of the saints, that might well have been the case; but there is little doubt that such a theocratic system would have weighed heavily on the mass of the people.

Both *A Standard Set Up* and *A Door of Hope* witnessed to the passionate preoccupation of the Fifth Monarchists with the abuses of the prevailing legal system. So that there should be a 'most equal and constant administration of justice' (*A Standard Set Up*), and that 'distributive justice might be equally administered between man and man, without respect for poor or rich, free or bond', and that a 'constant incorrupted course of justice might freely run down to all' (*A Door of Hope*), the introduction of a completely new legal system was envisaged.

A court of justice was to be set up in each county to deal with serious cases, both civil and criminal, and was to sit once every three months, or more frequently, if necessary. Other courts were to be set up in large towns and were to sit once a month, to deal with cases of lesser importance. There was to be a right of appeal from these to the county courts, and from the latter to the Supreme Council. The hated lawyers were to be done away with, for, *A Standard Set Up* promised, each man would be allowed to plead his own cause. It was conceded, however, that in difficult cases 'pleaders' might be employed as impartial helpers, 'to finde out the truth of the cause, and not to obscure and overthrow it, as has been too often seen'.

In these last bitter words was reflected the justified resentment of the Fifth Monarchists against the predatory lawyers of the time. Yet, though the proposals for an incorrupt and efficient legal system open to all were wholly admirable in theory, and embodied sensible reforms such as the abolition of the death sentence for theft, and modifications of the law concerning debtors, it is difficult to see how the new system could have proved a success in practice. For example, the proposal that each man should be his own lawyer would almost certainly have proved impracticable. The very framers of the reform seemed to have had some fear of this, hence their concession that in some cases special 'pleaders' might have to be called upon. Moreover, the judges of the new dispensation, giving verdicts according to the standards of the saints, would no doubt have provoked much discontent and opposition.

A Door of Hope claimed that if the new system were introduced the people of England would have 'magistrates like Job, that will be eyes to the blinde, and feet to the lame, and fathers to the poor, that will break the jaws of the wicked'. It was in the concluding words, surely, that the sting lay. The jaws of the wicked would be broken, indeed; but wickedness would be judged by the saints, and their standards, and criteria, were apt in many cases to be severe.

It is true that *A Standard Set Up* proclaimed that no man was to be committed or detained in prison without legal proceedings; that taxes should be levied only with the people's consent and in accordance with law; and that the Supreme Council should not 'violate, take away or enervate any of the foundations of common right and freedom which are or shall be agreed upon'. On the other hand, however, it added a clause, 'save in case of a further convincing light'—and therein lay the danger. If the saints should see such a light, that would be held justification enough for whatever changes were considered necessary.

In Church affairs the Fifth Monarchists were insistent that

tithes were to be abolished as 'antichristian and altogether in-
consistent with the gospel spirit' (*A Standard Set Up*). There
was to be no established church, and ministers were to be maintained either by the work of their own hands, or by voluntary
contributions from their flock. Though the prevailing system of
tithes was badly in need of reform, it is difficult to see how the
alternative means of maintaining the clergy envisaged by the
Fifth Monarchy Men would have proved satisfactory. In this, as
in other matters, they failed to put forward sufficiently detailed
and constructive remedies for the evils which they proposed to
abolish.

This weakness is also apparent in their approach to economic
affairs. All oppressions and grievances with regard to land
tenure, such as services, fines, rents, and profits of courts, were to
be 'abrogated and clean removed' (*A Standard Set Up*). But
there was no hint of compensation to be paid, however small, for
this extinction of rights which, however outdated and onerous,
were lawfully held. The excise, 'that wicked and unlawful oppression' (*A Standard Set Up*) and customs dues were to be
abolished; but no mention was made of how alternative revenues
were to be raised. Other economic reforms proposed were dealt
with in an equally superficial way. *A Door of Hope* stated that
'all the poor of the land might be set to work, and we might
have no beggars'; but left it at that, with no specific proposals for
putting the unemployed to useful labour. Other proposals were
set down in equally summary manner, and were, it would seem,
selected almost at random. Home industry and trade, *A Door of
Hope* stated, should be carefully protected, and so there must be
'no transporting of leather unwrought, fuller's earth, or other
commodities that may spoil the manufacture of the land, and im-
poverish the poor tradesman'; and the country's stock of timber
must be preserved and increased. Such bare, disjointed proposals
hardly constitute a coherent, constructive policy of economic reform, or even provide the framework for one.

This refusal to confront reality, and to consider the full political
and economic implications of their proposals, was of course due
to the millenarian faith. If the Kingdom was to be of Christ,
and guided by godly men ruled by divine precepts, then all would
be provided for. 'Seek ye first the Kingdom of God and his
righteousness; and all these things shall be added unto you'

(Matthew vi. 33). This injunction of Christ the Fifth Monarchy Men made their own, and it provided the basis for a comfortable philosophy which evaded the issues of practical politics.

Nevertheless, the promise of the coming millennium, when the country would be set on a new basis, and justice would be equally administered between man and man, without respect to poor or rich, bond or free, satisfied among the rank and file of the sect deeply-felt social and economic yearnings; and to this extent Fifth Monarchism, though primarily a religious movement, was also a product of the economic forces at work in seventeenth-century England.

The newly-emerging industrial proletariat could not fail to be stirred by a vision which seemed to promise social equality and economic betterment; and sometimes a Fifth Monarchy Man spoke to them in language which stressed this earthy, economic aspect of the faith. Thus on 22 April 1655 John Sanders, who was an ironmonger by trade, published a broadsheet entitled: 'An Iron Rod for the Naylors and Trades-men near Birmingham.'

Sanders spoke first to the employers:

Good friends and honest neighbours, and brothers of a trade [he said], to you at this time I chiefly address myself: What manner of persons ought we now to be, in all godliness and honesty of life, living in brotherly love one towards another! To which purpose I commend to you this course in our trade: and first I speake to you rich, covetous, and uncharitable ironmongers of mine own native country, and also to other trades and occupations in other countries. I am to charge you in the name of the living God whose workman-ship you are, that you be not highminded or uncharitable, grinding the faces of the poor, whom the Lord has promised to deliver for his name sake.... Live no longer like so many *Dives* keeping the poor like so many afflicted Lazarus's.... Amend your lives there-fore for the time to come, and live to that end God gave you a being, the generall good: give better prises, 2^d in 12^d, to poor workmen, that they may not have cause to hate you, many hundreds of them enjoying nothing but misery and want....

After this exhortation to the employers, Sanders gave to the workers advice which has a positively Marxist ring about it:

Brethren and fellow-sufferers [he declared], if this be not forthwith done, for the healing of your grievances, then take my counsel, let them work themselvs: for certainly you that make the ware are the most, and most considerable, though least valued and worst provided for.

Politically, in the light of the classic conception of democracy, the Fifth Monarchy Men were anti-democratic. Unlike the Levellers, who sought to establish the sovereignty of the people by means of a widely-diffused manhood suffrage, and elected parliaments, the Fifth Monarchy Men believed in rule by a narrow class. This was the elite of the nation, consisting of men of the 'choicest light and spirit', who alone were qualified by divine providence to choose the Sanhedrim or supreme Governing Council. The members of this elite were to be found exclusively in the various 'gathered churches' or independent congregations, and these 'God's freemen' were alone competent and authorized to choose the government of the nation, because of the divine grace with which God had endowed them.

It is true that in seeking to limit the foundation on which the edifice of government should be built, the Fifth Monarchy Men were in accord with the spirit of the age, for the traditional franchise had always been limited, both in the counties and the towns. Under the old system, however, there was at least voting, however narrowly and corruptly it might operate in practice. Moreover, the candidates for Parliament were not arbitrarily chosen by a very small religious minority, representing a minute part of the nation.

No doubt men chosen in the way favoured by the Fifth Monarchists might have proved, as the manifesto published by Venner in 1660 proclaimed, 'the best of men, of found principles, of known integrity, haters of bribes and covetousnesse'. It is far from certain, however, that because of this they would have been able, as Venner and his associates devoutly believed, to turn England into a 'well-ordered Commonwealth'. Such a Commonwealth it might well have proved, from the point of view of the saints, but not from that of the majority of the people. Therein lay the essential weakness of the political thinking of the Fifth Monarchy Men. They arrogantly equated the interests and desires of the nation as a whole with their own. If they had been able to attain supreme power, and keep it, they would have riveted upon England a system as bigoted and intolerant as any from which Englishmen had fought in the Civil War to free themselves.

The same bigotry and spiritual arrogance marked the policies advocated by the Fifth Monarchists in the field of foreign affairs. Their conception here was very simple. As soon as the saints had inaugurated the reign of King Jesus in England, they were, without pausing to rest under their vines and fig-trees (as *A Door of Hope* put it), to carry on the godly work by conquering France, Spain, Germany, and Rome itself, in order to bring these and all other nations into subjection to Christ. This fervent spirit even led the Fifth Monarchy Men to advocate the conquest of a Protestant nation, the Dutch.

In October 1653 members of the sect were preaching in London that if the war with the Dutch was brought to an end before victory was obtained, God's vengeance would follow on such a 'heathenish peace'. Where, the Fifth Monarchy Men asked, would they have a landing-place when they went to do the great work of the Lord, and tear the whore of Babylon out of her chair, if peace was made with a people and land which the Lord had already as good as given up wholly into the saints' hands?[7]

Although the Fifth Monarchy Men were not in general what in modern parlance would be called 'progressive' thinkers, in one question at least, the status of women, they showed an enlightened attitude which was unusual in an age which on the whole relegated women to a domestic and subordinate role. John Rogers, for example, devoted the whole of Chapter Eight of *Challah* (Book Two of his *Ohel or Bethshemesh*) to a consideration of the position of women in a Christian church. After quoting many passages of Scripture to prove that in the past women had often surpassed men in piety, judgement, and good deeds, he came to the conclusion that there was no justification for the superiority which men claimed. Therefore, Rogers said, in every church congregation the sisters ought to have equal rights with the brethren in speaking and in the general management of affairs—though he agreed that women could not be allowed to preach in public, or teach, as ministers did. He concluded that women's services, if properly used, would be of great benefit to the church and the nation; and he ended his chapter with the

---

[7] Thurloe, *State Papers*, Vol. I, p. 534.

following words of comfort and advice to the sisters: 'I wish ye be not too forward, and yet not too backward, but hold fast your liberty. . . . Your liberty with full sailes shall bring forth abundantly to serve all the country round!'

Other Fifth Monarchy Men seem to have shared Rogers' views, for women were allowed to play a considerable part in the affairs of the sect. Rogers and other leading members thought highly of and paid great deference to Hannah Trapnell, the prophetess; and another woman, Sister Hardy (or Harding), was given a special position of trust by Venner and his associates, for she was thought capable enough to be given the custody of the confidential papers.

Another sister, named Cary, even ventured to compete with the more literate and illustrious of the brethren as an author, and in 1651 published:

The Little Horns
Doom and Downfall:

or a

Scripture Prophesie

of

King James and King Charles,
and of this present Parliament
unfolded,
Wherein it appeares, that the late Tragedies
that have bin acted upon the Scene of
these three Nations: and particularly the
late Kings doom and death, was so long
ago, as by *Daniel* predeclared,

and

What the issue of all will be, is also
discovered; which followes in the second Part.

The book was dedicated to 'the vertuous heroicall and honourable ladies, the Lady Elizabeth Cromwel, the Lady Bridget Ireton, and the Lady Margaret Role'[8] because, so the writer said, they had acknowledged and maintained and defended all the truths proclaimed in the book. Hugh Peters, a prominent Puritan preacher, who was later executed as a regicide, contributed

---

[8] Bridget Ireton was Cromwell's eldest daughter. Margaret Role (or Rolle) was the wife of an eminent judge, Henry Rolle.

a commendatory foreword in which he observed that the authoress had:

taught her sexe that there are more ways than one to avoid idle-ness (the devils cushion) on which so many sit and sleep their last. They that will not use the distaff may improve a pen.... A holy, modest and painfull spirit runs through her endeavours.... In this dress you shall neither see naked brests, black patches, nor long trains; but an heart breathing after the coming of Christ, and the comfort of saints.

The views of the authoress were strictly orthodox, by the Fifth Monarchy canon. In the year 1656, she said, some glorious event would occur to bring about the deliverance, that was, the conversion of the Jews. She concluded:

How happy will he be that shall live five and forty years beyond that! For that is the utmost period of time that is set for the compleat deliverance of the holy people, the church, from all enemies whatsoever.... The great day will come at the period of the thousand, three hundred and five and thirty days.... In this year, or neer this year, 1701, I am persuaded that day will be!

In her preoccupation with the conversion of the Jews the authoress was giving expression to a belief held by most Fifth Monarchy Men, that the conversion of God's chosen people to Christianity was a necessary preliminary to Christ's return to earth to inaugurate the thousand-year rule of the saints. Christ's Kingdom, the Fifth Monarchy Men said, must comprise the tribes of the Israelites, as well as the Gentiles. This was in accord-ance with various texts. For example, Matthew xix. 27–28:

Then answered Peter and said unto him, Behold, we have forsaken all, and followed thee; what shall we have therefore?
And Jesus said unto them, Verily I say unto you, That ye which have followed me, in the regeneration when the Son of man shall sit in the throne of his glory, ye also shall sit upon twelve thrones, judging the twelve tribes of Israel.

The gloss put upon the last phrase was that 'judging' meant 'ruling'; and though it was conceded that ten of the tribes had been lost, it was confidently predicted that they would in due course be found, gathered in, and also made subjects of Christ's Kingdom. In fact, the Israelites would enjoy the greatest glory in the Kingdom, 'as the naturall branches of a stocke before a wild branch ingrafted; therefore it [Christ's Kingdom] is called the Kingdom of Israel, Acts i, 6, though it containe all saints'.[9]

The time appointed for the conversion of the Jews was said to be forecast in Daniel xii. 11–12:

And from the time that the daily sacrifice shall be taken away, and the abomination that maketh desolate set up, there shall be a thousand two hundred and ninety days. Blessed is he that waiteth, and cometh to the thousand three hundred and five and thirty days.

It was generally believed that the abomination that maketh desolate was set up by the Roman Emperor Julian the Apostate when he established heathenism during his reign, about A.D. 360–6. If, therefore, the thousand two hundred and ninety days (which were to be interpreted as years) were added to those two dates, the years 1650 and 1656 resulted; and those would be the years in which the Israelites would be delivered through being converted to Christianity.

For forty-five years afterwards, however, the twelve tribes would suffer great troubles; but to end them Christ would at last appear in person to begin his millennial reign with the saints. That, the Fifth Monarchy Men believed, was what Daniel meant when he said that those would be blessed who endured to the end of the thousand three hundred and five and thirty days.

The lengthy and laborious efforts of the sect to interpret the Bible in accordance with their preconceived ideas, and their insistence on the necessity of the conversion of the Jews, resulted in many Fifth Monarchy Men developing strong Hebraic tendencies and sympathies; and opponents sometimes commented caustically about this. Thus, for example, one Zachary Crofton, provoked by John Rogers' polemics in *Ohel or Bethshemesh*, published in 1653 a counterblast which he sarcastically entitled: 'Bethshemesh clouded, or Some animadversions on the rabbinical Talmud of Rabbi John Rogers.'

However, not everybody was impelled by such traditional animosity against the Jews; advocates of toleration also published their views. For instance, on 21 February 1649 Edward Nicholas published: 'An Apology for the Honorable Nation of the Jews and all the Sons of Israel.'

---

[9] H. Archer, *The Personall Reign of Christ upon Earth* (1642), p. 27.

Nicholas referred to the 'strict and cruel laws' enforced against the people whom God had chosen as his own; and he asserted that if the persecution continued, England would deprive itself of God's favour and protection. But apart from expediency, Nicholas also argued the case for toleration on ethical grounds.

It is not tollerable [he said] to adde affliction to the afflicted, as we do in continuing laws against them; it stands not with a generous spirit, to triumph over a man helpless and in misery . . . but rather that we endeavour to comfort them, and (if it were possible) to give them satisfaction for the innocent blood of theirs shed in the kingdom, and to restore them to commerce amongst us.

The upsurge of interest in the Jews among the English Puritans in general, and among the Fifth Monarchy Men in particular, encouraged Menasseh ben Israel, a Jewish rabbi in Amsterdam, to send in 1650 to the Parliament in England a pamphlet asking that favour and goodwill might be extended to the members of his faith. The Jews had been expelled from England as long ago as A.D. 1290, and though during the subsequent centuries individual Jews covertly re-entered the country, Edward I's decree of banishment was not rescinded, and this prevented Jews from openly settling in England and practising their faith.

The Fifth Monarchy Men were, however, anxious for the Jews to be readmitted to England, so that the conversion to Christianity could be effected, and the way thus made clear for Christ's return to establish his Kingdom. Cromwell, too, was sympathetic to Menasseh ben Israel's plea, though with him worldly motives predominated, even though the spirit of toleration was not lacking. To Cromwell the Jews would prove useful in a number of ways—as financial, commercial, and intelligence agents, because of their connexions throughout Europe.

Accordingly negotiations were opened with Menasseh ben Israel in 1651. It was not until 1655, however, that he was invited to come to London; but then, partly as a result of this visit, on 25 June 1656 the Council of State appears to have permitted once again the practice of the Jewish religion in England. The first step was thus taken towards the readmission of Jews, and their open participation in finance, trade, and industry.

Though the Fifth Monarchy Men undoubtedly played an

indirect part in bringing about this historic decision, that part must not be over-estimated, nor must their motives be misconstrued. Their interest in the Old Testament, and their insistence that the conversion of the Jews was an indispensable precondition of Christ's second coming undoubtedly helped to generate that revival of interest in the Jews which encouraged Menasseh ben Israel to make his approach to the new Puritan regime in England. To this extent the Fifth Monarchy Men can be said to have played a part in bringing about the readmission of the Jews to England. There can be little doubt, however, that Cromwell's pressing financial and commercial needs were much more influential in determining the Council of State's decision.

Similarly, reservations must be made about the motives of the Fifth Monarchy Men in pressing for the Jews' readmission. Though some of the sect may have been partly influenced by genuine idealism and human sympathy for the Jews, there can be little doubt that the spirit of pure religious toleration was not a determining factor in the attitude of the Fifth Monarchy Men. Religious toleration was not an article of their faith; and their advocacy of the Jews' return to England was as utilitarian as Cromwell's—though on a different basis. Cromwell wanted the Jews for the financial and commercial advantages which he hoped they would bring; the Fifth Monarchy Men wanted them as harbingers of the long-awaited Kingdom of Christ.

With regard to some other developments in the seventeenth century, apart from the admission of the Jews, the Fifth Monarchy Men can be said to have played a not unimportant part, thus influencing the subsequent course of English history. During the Civil War and Interregnum the Army and its leaders had frequently interfered in political affairs, and had consequently engendered a deep and widespread distrust and dislike of standing forces. After the Restoration this led to a decision to disband the Army; and Parliament adopted a plan by which the various regiments were to be broken up in succession, in an order to be determined by lot. As a concession to Monk, Duke of Albemarle, however, it was agreed that his own two regiments, of horse and foot, should be the last to be disbanded.

The plan was carried out with such efficiency that by January 1661 the turn of Monk's regiment of horse had come; but then Venner's revolt of 6 January caused the process to be halted. As a result of the fright occasioned by the Fifth Monarchy Men's insurrection a decision was taken to maintain in being, after all, a small force to protect the King and suppress any future attempts to overthrow the Government by force. Monk's two regiments were therefore not disbanded, and some new regiments were raised to form with them the force required. This body of men, which was small indeed compared with the New Model Army, but which was, however, a relic of that famous force 'barely saved from the ruins of a military government',[10] became the nucleus of the modern British Army, although it was not brought under parliamentary control until the passing of the Mutiny Act in 1689.

In the controversies which developed in England in the seventeenth century and led to the Civil War, two major elements can be discerned, one secular, the other religious. The first was the desire for parliamentary government, as expressed, for example, in a radical way by the Levellers; the other was reflected in the continuous, passionate debate on the nature of the church, and the part it should play in men's lives. The contention of the Fifth Monarchy Men that England should be ruled by an assembly of godly men chosen by the saints focused attention on both these burning issues of the age.

A body such as the saints had dreamed of came into being when Barebone's Parliament was convened; but the Fifth Monarchy minority in that assembly aroused such opposition among the conservatively-minded because of the radical reform proposals which were put forward, that the experiment of rule by the godly failed. Cromwell himself, in a speech to a committee of Parliament, on Tuesday, 21 April 1657, said so explicitly. After reviewing the course of events since the end of the Civil War, he referred to Barebone's Parliament, and said to the members of the committee: 'Truly, I will now come and tell you a story of my own weakness and folly. And yet it was done in my simplicity, I dare avow it was. . . .'

After the dismissal of the Rump, Cromwell continued, it was thought that 'men of our judgement, that had fought in the wars and were all of a piece on that account—why, surely these men

---

[10] Fortescue, *A History of the British Army* (London 1910), Vol. I, p. 310.

will hit it! Truly we did think, and I did think so; the more to blame. And such a company of men were chosen and did proceed into action. . . .'

Cromwell then recalled how the 'sober men' of Barebone's Parliament had withdrawn and voluntarily surrendered their mandate, since they had sincerely believed that if the assembly had continued to sit the result would have been 'the subversion of the laws and of all the liberties of this nation, in a word the confusion of all things, and, instead of order, to set up the judicial law of Moses in abrogation of all our administrations!'

Cromwell concluded by asserting that 'the persons that led in the meeting [i.e. Barebone's Parliament] were Mr. Feake and his meeting in Blackfriars, Major-General Harrison, and those that associated with him at one Mr. Squibb's house; and there were all the resolutions taken that were acted in that House day by day, and this was so *de facto*, I know it to be true!'[11]

Cromwell was disillusioned and dismayed by the policies advocated by the Fifth Monarchy Men in Barebone's Parliament; and they confirmed him in his naturally conservative attitude. There can be no doubt that his feelings were shared by a majority of the gentry and the commercial and industrial middle-classes, the classes who mattered. The memory of Barebone's Parliament remained vivid in these men's minds, and helped in no small way to swell that tide of conservative and traditional opinion which ultimately swept in the Restoration.

Ludlow in his *Memoirs* (Vol. II, p. 449) believed that Cromwell had no real sympathy for the Fifth Monarchy Men, but used them, particularly Major-General Harrison, as a means of getting rid of the Rump. Cromwell, said Ludlow, by professing millenarian beliefs 'absolutely fooled Harrison'; and a later writer, Edward Rogers, shared this belief.[12]

However, this is unjust to Cromwell. Though he did not believe in their religious doctrines, Cromwell regarded the Fifth Monarchy Men as godly and well-meaning, though misguided and therefore in need of control. It was in this spirit that he did

---

[11] Abbott, *The Writings and Speeches of Oliver Cromwell*, Vol. IV, p. 489.
[12] Rogers, *Some Account of the Life and Opinions of a Fifth Monarchy Man* (London 1867), p. 46.

not oppose the calling of Barebone's Parliament; and it was only when the political and economic ideas of the saints were revealed as potentially destructive of the existing order that Cromwell turned against them.

His change of attitude turned their plaudits into bitter invective, and incitements to revolt against the Protector and his regime. But although as a result Cromwell was forced to imprison the leading agitators, that was as far as he carried his punitive measures; and no Fifth Monarchy Man paid with his life for his opposition to the Lord Protector. In his dealings with the sect Cromwell was extremely patient and forbearing, despite continuous provocation; and this can only be explained by his conviction, expressed to John Rogers during the confrontation in Whitehall in February 1655, that despite all their extravagances, the preachers of the sect meant well and spoke 'many things according to the Gospel'.

At this distance in time it is difficult to share Cromwell's magnanimity, for generally speaking the Fifth Monarchy Men repel, rather than attract, both by their behaviour and their ideas. They were indeed, as the Lord God said of Israel (Exodus xxxiii. 3), 'a stiff-necked people'. Their chief spokesmen, such as Rogers and Feake, were devoid of a sense of humour, and were full of a feeling of self-pity for sufferings which they had largely brought upon themselves by their own intemperate language and foolish conduct. Like all bigots they were convinced of their own infallibility as members of a godly elect; but the means they chose to demonstrate this in word and deed were singularly inept.

It is true that the militant as opposed to the literary brethren had more to commend them. The bravery with which Harrison went to his death, and the extraordinary courage of Venner and his associates redeemed, to some extent, the spiteful verbosities and foolish antics of people like Rogers and Feake. Nevertheless it remains a tragedy that so much courage was expended on so futile a cause; for the political and economic ideas of the Fifth Monarchy Men, quite apart from their religious aberrations, were superficial and insubstantial as a blueprint for a new and better order of society.

Moreover, the dominating aim of the sect, that England should be governed by a Sanhedrim of godly men chosen arbitrarily according to preconceived conceptions of piety, ran clean contrary to the main current of political development in the country in the seventeenth century. This development was to lead in the end to the evolution of modern democratic ideas; but the views of the Fifth Monarchy Men were a harking-back to the medieval conception that religion should embrace and control every aspect of human life. In the sense that this conception was contrary to the tendency towards the secularization of political thought which had set in since the Reformation, the ideas of the Fifth Monarchy Men were not only unrealistic, but anachronistic also.

What then remains to be said in favour of the sect? One student of their activities, at least, has held that their ideal, however impracticable, is worthy of admiration. 'They held', he asserted (in 1905), 'an ideal which for purity and splendour is, when compared with those for which our generation gives its strength, as a Matterhorn among molehills!'[13]

This sentiment may have seemed impeccable in the age of Edwardian materialism. A later generation, however, with experience of the dictatorships which led to the outbreak of the Second World War, will have reservations to make about all militant minorities with ideals. That of the Fifth Monarchy Men may well have seemed pure and splendid in theory. In practice, however, it would have led to a monstrous tyranny over Englishmen; and those at the head of it would have striven fanatically and with grim determination to extend their tyranny overseas.

After the Civil War the traditional system of government under which Englishmen had lived for centuries collapsed; and many soon felt an acute sense of insecurity and discontent under the different regimes which succeeded it. The Fifth Monarchy Men, with their promises of the salvation to be brought by the advent of the thousand-year reign of Christ, offered an easy and enticing way out of present troubles to many simple folk who were poor and perplexed, and offered them, too, the swift removal of many abuses by which they were oppressed.

Tennyson's conception of freedom slowly broadening down from precedent to precedent may often have been used in the past to mask an obstinate reluctance by vested interests to surrender their privileges for the common good. There can be little

[13] C. H. Simpkinson, *Thomas Harrison, Regicide and Major-General* (London 1905), Editor's Preface, p. vi.

doubt, however, that the slow, pragmatic process of change is more in accordance with the English national temperament, than a sudden transformation imposed by force.

England, as her history shows, does not like revolutions; and the failure of the Fifth Monarchists and their cause did not result merely from the hostility of those who saw their own private or class interests threatened. Though some of the reforms and ideas advocated by the Fifth Monarchy Men were admirable, and though their intentions were honest and altruistic, the sect was unacceptable to the great majority of Englishmen because of the fanaticism and militancy of its extremists.

Their ideals may have been as lofty as a Matterhorn; but most Englishmen did not approve of the means proposed to reach the summit, and preferred, intuitively, to keep their feet planted firmly on the ground.

SOURCES

(Short titles only of seventeenth-century publications are given).

ABBOTT, W. C., *The Writings and Speeches of Oliver Cromwell* (4 Vols., Cambridge, Mass. 1937–47).

A Declaration of Major-General Harrison, Prisoner in the Tower of London (1660).

A Door of Hope (1660).

A Judgment and Condemnation of the Fifth Monarchy Men (1661).

A Narrative wherein is faithfully set forth the sufferings of John Cann (1658).

A Standard Set Up (1657).

A True Discovery of a Bloody Plot (1661).

A Witness to the Saints in England (1657).

An Advertisement as touching the Fanaticks Late Conspiracy (1661).

An Alarum to the City and Souldiery (1659).

ARCHER, H., *The Personall Reign of Christ upon Earth* (1642).

ASHLEY, M., *Cromwell's Generals* (London 1954).
    Oliver Cromwell and the Puritan Revolution (London 1958).

ASPINWALL, W., *A Brief Description of the Fifth Monarchy* (1653).
    An Explication and Application of the Seventh Chapter of Daniel (1654).
    A Premonition of Sundry Sad Calamities yet to Come (1654).
    The Legislative Power is Christ's Peculiar Prerogative (1656).

AUBREY, J., *Miscellanies* (4th Edition, London 1857).

BANKS, C. E., *Thomas Venner* (Boston, Mass. 1893).

BAXTER, R., *Reliquiae Baxterianae* (London 1696).

BESANT, W., *Westminster* (London 1895).

BIRCH, T., *A Collection of the State Papers of John Thurloe Esquire* (7 Vols., London 1742).

BLENCOWE, R. W., *The Sydney Papers* (London 1825).

BRAILSFORD, H. N., *The Levellers and the English Revolution* (London 1961).

BROWN, L. F., *The Political Activities of the Baptists and Fifth Monarchy Men in England during the Interregnum* (London 1912. Reissued New York 1965).

BRUNTON, D., and PENNINGTON, D. H., *The Members of the Long Parliament* (London 1954).

BRYANT, A., *King Charles II* (London 1955).

BURRAGE, C., *The Fifth Monarchy Insurrections* (in the *English Historical Review* Vol. XXV, London 1910).

Calendar of State Papers Domestic (1653–82).

Calendar of State Papers Venetian (1657–61).

CANNE, J., *A Seasonable Word to the Parliament Men* (1659).

The Time of the End (1657).

CARY, M., *A New and More Exact Mappe or Description of New Jerusalems Glory* (1651).

The Little Horns Doom and Downfall (1651).

Certain Quaeres Humbly Presented in Way of Petition by Many Christian People (1649).

Clarendon State Papers (3 Vols., Oxford 1767–86).

CLARKE, J., *The Plotters Unmasked* (1661).

COBBETT, W., *Complete Collection of State Trials* (Vol. VI, London 1810).

COHN, N., *The Pursuit of the Millennium* (London 1957).

CROFTON, Z., *Bethshemesh Clouded* (1653).

CROSS, F. L., *Oxford Dictionary of the Christian Church* (Oxford 1957).

DAVIES, D., *Vavasor Powell* (London 1896).

DAVIES, G., *The Early Stuarts* (Oxford 1959).

Dictionary of National Biography.

ELMES, J., *A Topographical Dictionary of London* (London 1831).

EVANS, A., *The Bloudy Vision of John Farly* (1655).

The Voice of the Iron Rod (1655).

EVELYN, J., *Diary* (6 Vols., Oxford 1955).

FEAKE, C., *A Beam of Light* (1659).

The Oppressed Close Prisoner in Windsor Castle (1654).

FIRTH, C. H., *The Clarke Papers* (4 Vols., Camden Society, London 1891–1901).

The Last Years of the Protectorate (2 Vols., London 1909).

Memoir of Major-General Thomas Harrison (Worcester, Mass. 1893).

The Memoirs of Edmund Ludlow (2 Vols., Oxford 1894).

Oliver Cromwell (Oxford 1958).

FIXLER, M., *Milton and the Kingdoms of God* (London 1964).

FORTESCUE, J. W., *A History of the British Army* (Vol. I, London 1910).

GARDINER, S. R., *History of the Commonwealth and Protectorate* (3 Vols., London 1894).

History of the Great Civil War (4 Vols., London 1893).

GLASS, H. A., *The Barbone Parliament* (London 1899).

GOOCH, G. P., *Political Thought in England from Bacon to Halifax* (London 1927).

GOODWIN, T., *A Sermon of the Fifth Monarchy* (1654).

HALL, T., *Chiliastomastix Redivivus* (1657).

HALLER, W., *Liberty and Reformation in the Puritan Revolution* (New York 1955).

HARBEN, H. A., *A Dictionary of London* (London 1918).

HASTINGS, J., *Dictionary of the Bible* (2nd edition, revised by F. C. Grant and H. H. Rowley, Edinburgh 1963).

HEARNSHAW, F. J. C., *The Life of Sir Henry Vane* (London 1910).

HEATH, J., *Flagellum, or the Life and Death, Birth and Burial, of Oliver Cromwell, the Late Usurper* (2nd edition, London 1663).

HERBERT, T., *Memoirs of the Two Last Years of the Reign of King Charles I* (4th edition, London 1839).

HEXTER, J. H., *Reappraisals in History* (London 1961).

HILL, C., *The Century of Revolution* (London 1961).
The Barebones Parliament: A Revaluation (in *The Listener*, 23 July 1953).
Puritanism and Revolution (London 1958).
Society and Puritanism in Pre-Revolutionary England (London 1964).

Historical MSS. Commission (MSS. of Earl of Lonsdale; A. G. Finch; S. H. Le Fleming; F. W. Leyborne-Popham; Marquess of Ormonde).

HOBMAN, D. L., *Cromwell's Master Spy* (London 1961).

HOWES, E., *Annales, or a Generall Chronicle of England Begun by John Stow, continued and augmented with Matters Foraigne and Domestique, Ancient and Moderne, unto the end of this present yeere* (London 1631).

HYDE, E., (Earl of Clarendon) *History of the Rebellion and Civil Wars in England* (6 Vols., Oxford 1888).

HUTCHINSON, J., *Memoirs of the Life of Colonel Hutchinson, Governor of Nottingham, by his widow Lucy* (Revised by C. H. Firth, London 1906).

INDERWICK, F. A., *Side Lights on the Stuarts* (London 1888).

JAMES, M., *Social Problems and Policy during the Puritan Revolution* (London 1930).

JONES, R. M., *Mysticism and Democracy in the English Commonwealth* (Cambridge, Mass. 1932).

KAUFMAN, R, *Millénarisme et Acculturation* (Brussels 1964).

KNOTT, C. G., *Napier Tercentenary Memorial Volume* (Edinburgh 1915).

LIPMAN, V. D., *Three Centuries of Anglo-Jewish History* (London 1961).

Londons Glory (1661).

MACOMBER, H. P., *Glimpses of the Human Side of Sir Isaac Newton* (New York 1955).

MCELWEE, W., *England's Precedence* (London 1956).

MCLACHLAN, H., *The Religious Opinions of Milton, Locke, and Newton* (*Manchester* 1941).

MONTAGUE, F. C., *History of England: From the Accession of James I to the Restoration* (London 1929).

MORE, J., *A Trumpet Sounded: or the Great Mystery of the Two Little Horns Unfolded* (1654).
The Second Sounding of the Little Horn (1654).

MORE, L. T., *Isaac Newton* (London 1934).

NAPIER, M., *Memoirs of John Napier of Merchiston* (Edinburgh 1834).

NEWTON, I., *Observations upon the Prophecies of Daniel and the Apocalypse of St. John* (London 1733).

NICHOLAS, E., *An Apology for the Honorable Nation of the Jews* (1649).

OGG, D., *England in the Reign of Charles II* (2 Vols., Oxford 1963).

ORR, J., *The International Standard Bible Encyclopaedia* (Chicago 1930).

PAGITT, E., *Heresiography* (London 1662).

PARES, R., and TAYLOR, A. J. P., *Essays Presented to Sir Lewis Namier* (London 1956).

PAUL, R. S., *The Lord Protector* (London 1955).

PENNEY, N., *The Journal of George Fox* (2 Vols., Cambridge 1911).

PEPYS, S., *Diary* (edited by Lord Braybrooke, Chandos Library Edition, London 1869).

PETEGORSKY, D. W., *Left Wing Democracy in the English Civil War* (London 1940).

Rebellion Unmasked (1661).

ROGERS, E., *Some Account of the Life and Opinions of a Fifth Monarchy Man* (London 1867).

ROGERS., J., *A Christian Concertation* (1659).
　Dod or Chathan (1653).
　Jegar-Sahadutha (1657).
　Mene, Tekel, Perez (1654).
　Ohel or Bethshemesh (1653).
　Sagrir (1653).
　To His Excellency the Lord General Cromwell (1653).

ROSS, A., *A View of all Religions in the World* (London 1675).

ROTH, C., *A History of the Jews in England* (Oxford 1964).

ROUTH, M. J., *Bishop Burnet's History of His Own Time* (6 Vols., Oxford 1823).

RUSSELL, D. S., *The Method and Message of Jewish Apocalyptic 200 B.C.–A.D.100* (London 1964).

SANDERS, J., *An Iron Rod for the Naylors and Trades-men neer Birmingham* (1655).

SIMPKINSON, C. H., *Thomas Harrison, Regicide and Major-General* (London 1905).

SPITTLEHOUSE, J., *An Answer to one part of the Lord Protector's Speech* (1654).
　A Warning-Piece Discharged (1653).
　Certain Queries Propounded to the Most Serious Consideration (1654).
　The First Addresses to the Lord General (1653).

TAWNEY, R. H., *Religion and the Rise of Capitalism* (London 1926).

The Banner of Truth Displayed (1656).

The Downfall of the Fifth Monarchy (1657).

The Faithfull Narrative of the Late Testimony and Demand (1655).

The Fifth Monarchy or Kingdom of Christ in Opposition to the Beast's Asserted (1659).

The Indictment, Arraignment, Tryal and Judgment at large of Twenty-Nine Regicides, the Murtherers of his Most Sacred Majesty King Charles I of Glorious Memory (London 1739).

The Last Farewel to the Rebellious Sect called the Fifth Monarchy Men (1661).

The Phanatiques Creed (1661).

The Plotters Unmasked (1661).

The Prophets Malachy and Isaiah Prophecying to the Saints (1656).

The Traytors Tragedy (1660).

The Traytors Unvailed (1661).

THURLOE, J., *State Papers, see* BIRCH, T.

TREVELYAN, G. M., *England under the Stuarts* (London 1949).

TREVOR-ROPER, H. R., *Oliver Cromwell and His Parliaments* (in *Essays Presented to Sir Lewis Namier*, edited R. Pares and A. J. P. Taylor, London, 1956).

VANE, H., *A Healing Question Propounded and Resolved* (1656).

The Retired Man's Meditations (1655).

VARLEY, F. J., *Highgate Episodes: The Insurrection of Thomas Venner* (London 1938).

Major-General Thomas Harrison (London 1939).

VAUGHAN, R., *The Protectorate of Oliver Cromwell* (2 Vols., London 1838).

WALFORD, E., and THORNBURY, G. W., *Old and New London* (6 Vols., London 1873–8).

Water upon the Flame (1659).

WEDGWOOD, H. C., *The Life of Major-General Harrison* (Newcastle-under-Lyme 1880).

WHEATLEY, H. B., *London Past and Present* (3 Vols., London 1891).

WHITELOCKE, B., *Memorials of the English Affairs* (London 1732).

WHITING, C. E., *Studies in English Puritanism from the Restoration to the Revolution* (London 1931).

WOLF, L., *Menasseh Ben Israel's Mission to Oliver Cromwell* (London 1901).

YULE, G., *The Independents in the English Civil War* (Cambridge 1958).

ZAGORIN, P., *A History of Political Thought in the English Revolution* (London 1954).

INDEX